DK EYE

W9-BVH-451

TOP **10**
NEW ENGLAND

Top 10 New England Highlights

The Top 10 of Everything

CONTENTS

New England Area by Area

Streetsmart

Within each Top 10 list in this book, no hierarchy of quality or popularity is implied. All 10 are, in the editor's opinion, of roughly equal merit.

Throughout this book, floors are referred to in accordance with American usage; i.e., the "first floor" is at ground level.

Title page, front cover and spine *Picturesque Montpelier, Vermont, in fall*
Back cover, clockwise from top left *Skiing in New Hampshire; a church nestled in the Green Mountains, Vermont; Brightly lit city of Boston; Montpelier, Vermont; Bass Harbor Head lighthouse, Mount Desert Island, Maine*

The rapid rate at which the world is changing is constantly keeping the DK Eyewitness team on our toes. While we've worked hard to ensure that this edition of New England is accurate and up-to-date, we know that opening hours alter, standards shift, prices fluctuate, places close and new ones pop up in their stead. So, if you notice we've got something wrong or left something out, we want to hear about it. Please get in touch at **travelguides@dk.com**

Welcome to
New England

Scenic New England offers nature, history, and cutting-edge culture in abundance. Vibrant cities buzz with hip bars, intriguing museums, and fine dining restaurants. Beyond these urban centers, mountain trails skirt the horizon and brilliant fall foliage blankets the region in color. With DK Eyewitness Top 10 New England, it's yours to explore.

New England is admired for its oceanfront that ranges from the rockbound coast of Maine, with its endless inlets and spruce-tufted islands, to the sandy beaches of **Cape Cod National Seashore**. In Massachusetts, find the Boston Symphony on the summer lawns of **Tanglewood** in the **Berkshires**. In Connecticut, explore the historic vessels of **Mystic Seaport** and the waterfall-dotted **Litchfield Hills**. Cruise aboard an America's Cup yacht or marvel at the Gilded Age mansions in **Newport**, Rhode Island. The **Green Mountains** of Vermont and the **White Mountains** of New Hampshire glow with colors in the fall, entice through the summer with rivers for rafting and canoeing, and feature some of America's best skiing in winter.

History lives in the countryside around Boston, and factory outlet centers in every state sing their siren song to shoppers. Colorful and tasty festivals abound, from the **Maine Lobster Festival** to Boston's **Independence Day** concert and fireworks.

Whether you're coming for a week or a month, our Top 10 guide brings together the best of everything New England offers, from the pristine woods and shores of **Mount Desert Island** to the chic and sophisticated bars and restaurants of **Boston**. The guide has useful tips throughout, from seeking out what's free to finding places off the beaten track, plus eight easy-to-follow itineraries, designed to tie together a clutch of sights in a short span of time. Add inspiring photography and detailed maps, and you've got the essential pocket-sized travel companion. **Enjoy the book, and enjoy New England**.

Clockwise from top: Acadia National Park (Maine); *Friendship of Salem*, Salem Maritime National Historic Site (Massachusetts); Martha's Vineyard (Massachusetts); Block Island (Rhode Island); Boston Freedom Trail symbol; Lake Waramaug (Connecticut); Sunday River (Maine)

Exploring New England

New England packs extremes into a small area – from mountain wilderness to beaches that reach the horizon, from picturesque villages to pulsing cities. Start with two days on foot seeing the historic sights of Boston, then pack the car and head out to explore the rest of New England over the next seven days.

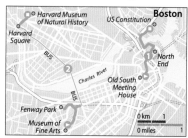

afternoon, spend some time exploring the historic village of **Stockbridge** (see p33) in the **Berkshires** (see pp32–3) and visit the hip town of **Great Barrington** (see p33). For the evening, buy advance tickets for the Boston Symphony (summer only) at **Tanglewood Music Center** (see p33).

Two Days in Boston

Day ❶
MORNING
Take a free Boston Park Ranger walking tour of sites along the **Freedom Trail** (see p13). Don't miss the Old South Meeting House.
AFTERNOON
Have lunch in the North End, Boston's version of Little Italy, before crossing the bridge to the USS Constitution (see p13).

Day ❷
MORNING
Start your day with Impressionism and more at Boston's **Museum of Fine Arts** (see p40).
AFTERNOON
Take a tour of Fenway Park (see p12) before heading to Harvard Square and the **Harvard Museum of Natural History** (see p43).

Seven Days in New England

Day ❶
Tour scenic **Lake Waramaug** (see p24) in the **Litchfield Hills** (see pp24–5), and climb the trail to the top of **Kent Falls** (see p24). Later in the

Day ❷
In the **Green Mountains** (pp 26–7), visit **Manchester's** (see p27) outlet stores and enjoy the breathtaking views from the **Mount Equinox Skyline Drive** (see p27). Tour **Hildene** (see p26), then drive to the stunning **Lakes Region** (see pp30–31) in New Hampshire.

Day ❸
At the resort of **Weirs Beach** (see p30), explore **Lake Winnipesaukee** (see p30) on board the **M/S Mount Washington** (see p30). Then drive north to Lincoln to follow the **Kancamagus Highway** (see p20) east, stopping for a hike to one of the many waterfalls. Continue east to **Portland** (see pp28–9).

Day ❹
Take a stroll around Portland's **Old Port District** (see p28) and enjoy a seafood lunch. Afterwards, drive to

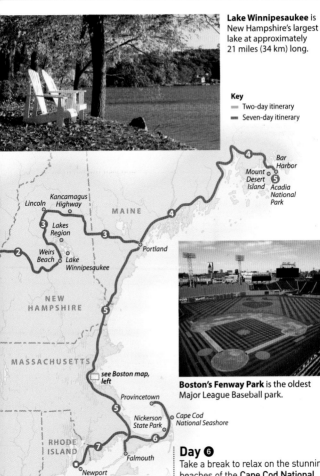

Lake Winnipesaukee is New Hampshire's largest lake at approximately 21 miles (34 km) long.

Key

— Two-day itinerary
— Seven-day itinerary

Boston's Fenway Park is the oldest Major League Baseball park.

the magical **Mount Desert Island** (*see pp14–15*) and visit the lively resort town of **Bar Harbor** (*see p14*) and the **Abbe Museum** (*see p15*).

Day ❺

Start the day by exploring the natural wonders of **Cadillac Mountain, Sand Beach**, and **Thunder Hole** (*see p15*) at Acadia National Park. Lunch early on the lawns at Jordan Pond House (*see p14*). Then drive south to **Cape Cod** (*see pp16–17*), stopping to visit the pretty town of **Falmouth** (*see p17*).

Day ❻

Take a break to relax on the stunning beaches of the **Cape Cod National Seashore** (*see p16*). In the late afternoon, head up to the colorful **Provincetown** (*see p17*) to enjoy its carnival atmosphere and, later, a fine-dining al fresco meal.

Day ❼

Rent a bike to explore the **Cape Cod Rail Trail** (*see p17*) and **Nickerson State Park** (*see pp18–19*), marvel at the sumptuous Gilded Age mansion **The Breakers** (*see p18*). Then admire Newport Harbor on an **America's Cup Charters** cruise (*see p18*).

Top 10 New England Highlights

Stowe Community Church nestled in
the Green Mountains, Vermont

TOP 10 New England Highlights

New England is an all-season destination of pine-scented mountains, ocean villages, urban centers – and so much more. It's also the birthplace of America, a fact attested by historic homes and museums. For many, the region is white churches, covered bridges, snowy ski slopes, blazing fall foliage, lighthouses on craggy cliffs, and lobsters fresh from the sea.

① Historic Boston
The American past is palpable in New England's largest city, where cobbled streets echo with the calls of patriots and cafés enliven the old Quincy Market *(see pp12–13)*.

② Mount Desert Island, Maine
Rugged headlands above a crashing ocean, hiking trails crisscrossing pine forests, and still ponds reflecting the sky's blue bowl express nature in all its unbounded wildness *(see pp14–15)*.

③ Cape Cod, Massachusetts
The bent arm of Cape Cod is a world of untamed dunes, bird-filled marshes, and quirky towns where visitors can savor fresh fish and sticky taffy *(see pp16–17)*.

Newport, Rhode Island ④
Opulent mansions on seaside cliffs reveal the splendors of the Gilded Age in this storied yachting harbor *(see pp18–19)*.

5 White Mountains, New Hampshire

Summer hikers and winter skiers relish these rugged, forested mountains. Hike, drive, or ride the cog railway up Mount Washington *(see pp20–21)*.

6 Litchfield Hills, Connecticut

Bistros and boutiques fill the white clapboard buildings of hill-country villages in this area where the rich keep country retreats *(see pp24–5)*.

7 Green Mountains, Vermont

From pre-Revolutionary villages to ridgeline hiking trails, the Green Mountains form the spine of Vermont. In fall, its forests blaze with color; in winter, some of the nation's top slopes lure skiers *(see pp26–7)*.

8 Portland and Casco Bay, Maine

Portland remains a seafaring center on a picturesque bay, but the Old Port also hosts galleries, inns, and boutiques *(see pp28–9)*.

9 Lakes Region, New Hampshire

Lake Winnipesaukee, with its 240-mile (386-km) shoreline, rules the region's kingdom of mountain-rimmed lakes *(see pp30–31)*.

10 Berkshires, Massachusetts

In summer, theater, music, and dance flourish in the Berkshire Hills. Lavish estates of a bygone era's millionaires lend a sophisticated air to homespun country villages here *(see pp32–3)*.

🔟⭐ Historic Boston

Founded in 1630 by Puritans who envisioned their settlement as a shining beacon to the world, Boston was among America's first great urban centers. Its patriots led the rebellion that grew into the American Revolution, and few places in the US evoke so vividly the birth of a nation. Centuries later, Boston remains at the national forefront in politics, the arts, culture, education, and science. It retains its Classical proportions, with modern buildings nudging up against landmarks of the Colonial and Revolutionary eras.

1 Massachusetts State House
Completed in 1798, this legislative temple with its ornate marble and paneled halls was architect Charles Bulfinch's masterpiece, and the model for capitols around the country **(below)**.

Map of Historic Boston

3 Black Heritage Trail
Boston's free African American community helped lead the nation in struggles to abolish slavery and achieve equal rights. The trail ends at the African Meeting House.

5 Granary Burying Ground
Some of Boston's most famous characters are buried at this Tremont Street graveyard of more than 2,300 slate tomb-stones in the shadow of downtown skyscrapers.

4 Boston Common and Public Garden
Concerts and Shakespeare plays enliven the Common, Boston's green heart since 1634. Tens of thousands of flowers bloom in the Public Garden, while Swan Boats glide on its pond **(below)**.

2 Fenway Park
All baseball fans long to see a game in Fenway. Opened in 1912, this is the oldest Major League Baseball park, and a shrine to the game.

6 Faneuil Hall

One of Boston's most significant Revolutionary sites, Faneuil Hall heard firebrands like Samuel Adams call for revolt against the king. The hall was partly funded by the slave trade and debate still rages over renaming it.

9 Old North Church

The spare decor typical of a Colonial house of worship barely hints at the fame of Christ Church **(above)**, where lanterns hung in its belfry signaled British troop movements.

THIS WAY TO HISTORY

The Freedom Trail (a red line on the sidewalk, either paint or bricks) snakes through Boston highlighting important sites of Colonial and Revolutionary history. The 2.5-mile (4-km) walking trail begins at Boston Common and ends with climbing Bunker Hill Monument in Charlestown. Pick up a map and inquire about free, ranger-led Freedom Trail tours at the Boston National Historical Park visitor center at Faneuil Hall (www.nps.gov/bost).

10 Harvard Yard

Free student-led tours through Harvard Yard **(below)** provide an insight into life at America's first and most prestigious university, founded in 1636.

7 Paul Revere House

Revere's house, built around 1680, is the oldest in Boston. During a visit here you get an intimate look at the domestic life of this key figure in the history of the American Revolution.

8 USS Constitution

Newly restored, USS Constitution is the world's oldest commissioned warship. The three-masted frigate, also known as "Old Ironsides," has served in the US Navy since 1797, battling North African pirates and foreign navies alike.

NEED TO KNOW

Massachusetts State House: **MAP W3**; 24 Beacon St

Fenway Park: **MAP S5**; 4 Jersey St

African Meeting House: **MAP V3**; 8 Smith Ct

Boston Common and Public Garden: **MAP V4**

Granary Burying Grounds: **MAP W3**

Faneuil Hall: **MAP X3**; Dock Sq

Paul Revere House: **MAP X3**; 19 North Sq

USS Constitution: **MAP W1**; Charlestown Navy Yard, 1 Constitution Rd, Charlestown

Old North Church: **MAP X2**; 193 Salem St

Harvard Yard: **MAP S1**

■ Security is tight at the USS Constitution. Bring photo ID and don't carry anything you couldn't take on an airplane.

■ Quincy Market food court, adjacent to Faneuil Hall, offers good variety and value for a quick lunch.

TOP 10 ⭐ Mount Desert Island, Maine

Mount Desert Island condenses the fabled Maine coast and woods into a single magical spot. Salt-splashed fishing villages dot the southwest lobe, while Bar Harbor on the east bustles with lodging options and restaurants. Painters of the 19th-century Hudson River School were among the first to celebrate Mount Desert's wild natural beauty, and their art encouraged wealthy industrialists to build summer estates thoughtfully incorporated into natural settings. Half the island falls within Acadia National Park.

1 Jordan Pond House

For a touch of gentility in the wilderness, nothing beats sitting in Adirondack chairs on the grassy lawn of the Jordan Pond House, where you can enjoy their famous popovers with afternoon tea.

2 Carriage Roads

To preserve auto-free tranquility, John D. Rockefeller Jr. built 45 miles (72 km) of carriage roads through land he gave to Acadia National Park – still reserved for hikers, cyclists, skiers, and equestrians.

3 Bar Harbor

Grand mansions line the shore of this lively resort town on Frenchman Bay. Bar Harbor (above) functions as a tourist center for the island. It's also a convenient base for visiting Acadia National Park.

4 Bass Harbor Head

At the southern tip of Mount Desert, Bass Harbor Head (below) towers above the sea. The lighthouse offers amazing views over the deep blue ocean.

NEED TO KNOW

MAP R3

Acadia National Park Visitor Center: off Rte 3, Hulls Cove; 207 288 3338, 877 444 6777 (camping reservations); open Apr–Jun & Sep–Oct: 8:30am–4:30pm daily; Jul–Aug: 8am–6pm daily; adm; www.nps.gov/acad

Jordan Pond House: Park Loop Rd, Seal Harbor; 207 276 3316; open May–late Oct: 11am–9pm daily; www.jordan pondhouse.com

Abbe Museum: 26 Mount Desert St, Bar Harbor; 207 288 3519; open May–Oct: 10am–5pm daily; Nov–Apr: 10am–4pm Thu–Sat; closed Jan; adm; www. abbemuseum.org

■ Acadia National Park is one of the most visited parks in the National Park system. For summer visits, reserve lodgings well in advance.

■ Check out Trenton Bridge Lobster Pound (see p130).

5 Cadillac Mountain
It's worth rising early to hike or drive up 1,527-ft (465-m) Cadillac Mountain **(above)** to catch the first rays of the sun to strike the US.

Map of Mount Desert Island

6 Thunder Hole
Swift tides and strong waves pounding the craggy ledges at Thunder Hole force air and water into a deep crease beneath the rock. Under the right conditions, a ground-shaking thunderclap echoes from the hole.

7 Southwest Harbor
This snug harbor, tucked inside two lobes of Mount Desert Island, is delightfully tranquil and picturesque. Take a lobster-hauling boat ride or catch the Cranberry Isles ferry here.

8 Abbe Museum
Explore 10,000 years of Native American culture in this museum devoted to the heritage of Maine's Wabanaki peoples. See basketry **(left)** and wood-carving at this modern museum in downtown Bar Harbor.

9 Hiking Trails
To penetrate the deep wilderness or get up close and personal with the mountains of Acadia National Park, use the network of more than 120 miles (193 km) of trails. They range from easy to very strenuous.

10 Sand Beach
Rugged cliffs and jumbled ledges line most of Acadia's shoreline, but thousands of visitors flock to this 870-ft (265 m) stretch of sandy cove **(below)** to sunbathe. Swimming is bracing, as the ocean water rarely exceeds 55º F (15º C).

🏆10 ⭐ Cape Cod, Massachusetts

Race Point at the tip of Cape Cod feels like the end of the earth. Beyond this long, thin crook of glacial sand lies the broad Atlantic, stretching all the way to Portugal. The Cape's fishing fleets haul the sweetest scallops and richest tuna; virtually every cove harbors a hamlet founded by farmers whose grandchildren turned to the sea. Great Beach extends for 30 miles (48 km), from Chatham to Provincetown, comfortably accommodating the thousands of swimmers and sunbathers who flock here during the summer.

① Sandwich Town Beach and Boardwalk

Gentle waves and warm waters make Town Beach excellent for children. It can be accessed from Cape Cod Canal while the boardwalk is being rebuilt (due to finish late 2023).

② Hyannis

Thanks to its airport and two ferry lines to Nantucket and Martha's Vineyard, Hyannis is Cape Cod's market town and transportation hub.

③ Cape Cod Canal

Dug to save ships from the perilous Nantucket Shoals, the canal marks the Cape's sedate beginning (below). Bike down its paths or fish for bass and ferocious bluefish.

④ Cape Cod National Seashore Beaches

Beaches for swimmers, kite-flyers, surfers, and sunbathers stretch from Nauset Beach to Race Point, with its historic Life-Saving Station (above).

⑤ Nickerson State Park

Clear glacial kettle ponds dot this wooded parkland far removed, physically and ecologically, from the Cape's shores. Canoe and fish the ponds, watch rare songbirds, and camp at over 400 sites.

Map of Cape Cod

6 Chatham

An iconic lighthouse marks the dangerous shoals off Chatham's astounding and ever-shifting barrier beaches, where seabirds flock and seals bask in the winter sun. Home to the Cape's main tuna fleet, Chatham is also a yachtsmen's harbor.

7 King's Highway

More shady lane than highway, Route 6A strings together the salty Cape Cod Bay villages filled with the mansions of Victorian sea captains, antiques dealers, and the studios of potters, glassblowers, and other artisans.

8 Cape Cod Rail Trail

This is one of the most invigorating ways to see Cape Cod. The 22-mile (35-km) Rail Trail begins in Dennis, crosses fields and forest, skirts a quaint fishing harbor, and then follows dune cliffs into Wellfleet.

9 Provincetown

It's always party time in P-town (left). The Cape's most colorful community is at once a Portuguese-American fishing village, a major art colony, and a leading gay resort destination.

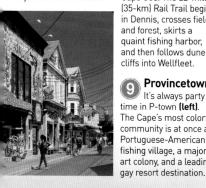

10 Falmouth and Woods Hole

The tiny research village of Woods Hole (above) and Falmouth proper, a quintessential New England town of neat houses and tall churches, are connected by Shining Sea bike path.

TOP 10 ⭐ Newport, Rhode Island

This small city packs a huge amount of history into a few square miles. Not only does it boast America's first naval college and first synagogue, its White Horse Tavern has been serving drinks since 1673. In the late 1800s, the rich began building ornate mansions along the cliffs south of the city center to escape fetid summers in New York. The New York Yacht Club made Newport its summer headquarters, and the city's harbor is home to many contenders for the America's Cup, the most prestigious match race in sailing.

1 The Breakers
Explore the gilt- and marble-encrusted interior of this 70-room Italian Renaissance-style mansion, completed in 1895, to appreciate the preeminence of the Vanderbilt family – who called it home – among the economic aristocracy of America.

2 Museum of Newport History
Artifacts and displays inside the Brick Store trace the merchants, patriots, craftsmen, and social elite of Newport with an emphasis on the 18th and 19th centuries.

4 Cliff Walk
The exhilarating amble (above) along Newport's east-facing cliffs will have you looking two ways at once – up to the lawns of the mansions on Bellevue Avenue and down to watch surfers catching waves at Easton's Beach.

6 Fort Adams State Park
The windy point between Newport Harbor and the Narragansett Bay East Passage is perfect for watching racing sailboats or flying kites. Newport's famous jazz and folk festivals are held here.

5 America's Cup Charters Cruises
Enjoy Newport Harbor's beauty from the deck of a racing yacht (below) that once competed for the America's Cup. You may even get to take the wheel.

3 Washington Square
Colonial-era Newport's focal point was damaged but not destroyed by British occupiers during the American Revolution. The first R.I. state house (above) heads the square.

7 Rose Island and Lighthouse
Volunteers man this historic lighthouse **(above)** a mile offshore from Newport. Experienced paddlers kayak to the island for excellent birding.

NEWPORT REGATTA
Usually held in mid-July, the Newport Regatta features racing in over 20 "One-Design" classes, where North American boats compete against others of like design. Sailing is only half the fun – the regatta is the highlight of the summer social season that starts at the marinas and spills over into the lively bars and restaurants.

NEED TO KNOW
MAP F5

Newport Visitor Information Center: 21 Long Wharf Mall; 401 845 9123; open daily

The Breakers: 44 Ochre Point Ave; 401 847 1000; open daily; adm

Museum of Newport History: 127 Thames St; 401 841 8770; open daily; adm

America's Cup Charters: 401 849 5868; open May–Oct; adm

Fort Adams State Park: Harrison Ave; 401 847 2400; open daily

Rose Island Lighthouse: 401 847 4242; open daily late May–mid-Oct; adm

Touro Synagogue: 85 Touro St; 401 847 4794; call for tour times; adm

International Tennis Hall of Fame: 194 Bellevue Ave; 401 849 3990; open daily (Jan–Mar: closed Tue); adm

■ An inexpensive RIPTA trolley day pass is the best way to see Newport.

■ Look for a truck selling Del's Lemonade along Thames Street or at Fort Adams State Park.

Map of Newport

9 International Tennis Hall of Fame
Play on the grass courts where US tournament tennis was born in 1881. The Hall still hosts professional matches, while the excellent museum chronicles the sport.

8 Touro Synagogue
The oldest synagogue in America, the spare and elegant Touro Synagogue was constructed in 1763 by religious refugees from Spain and Portugal.

10 Bowen's Wharf
You could develop a nautical swagger walking Bowen's Wharf, the anchor of Newport's waterfront activity since 1760. Head here for sail or powerboat tours, shopping at boutiques, or casual and fine dining.

TOP 10 ★ White Mountains, New Hampshire

More than 20 summits topping 4,000 ft (1,200 m) define the rugged north country of New Hampshire, of which 1,200 sq miles (3,116 sq km) is set aside as the White Mountain National Forest. The area is ideal for some of the main outdoor activities of New England: summer hiking and climbing, fall foliage sightseeing, and winter skiing. Drive through the White Mountains to encounter soaring mountain ridges, tumbling waterfalls, deep glens, and dark forests. Wildlife abounds – be careful of deer and moose on the roads at dusk.

1 Franconia Notch State Park

Stop along this 8-mile (13-km) pass between the Franconia and Kinsman mountain ranges to hike the challenging trails of the narrow-cut Flume Gorge, with its steep rock walls and gushing waterfalls.

3 Mount Washington and the Cog Railway

New England's highest peak at 6,288 ft (1,917 m), Mount Washington has lured climbers and sightseers since the 1840s. For the most picturesque ascent, take a 3-hour round trip on the Cog Railway (right), operating since 1869.

4 Conway Scenic Railroad

See the scenery as earlier generations did – from a train. Go through Mount Washington Valley, or over the towering trestles of Crawford Notch.

2 Kancamagus Highway

One of few roads across the spine of the White Mountains, the 34-mile (55-km) "Kanc" is among the state's most thrilling drives (see p54). Park the car and get out at the designated scenic areas (above) to picnic, hike, or explore Colonial history.

NEED TO KNOW

MAP L3–4, M3–4

Franconia Notch State Park Flume Gorge and Visitor Center: 603 745 8391; open mid-May–mid-Oct: daily; adm

White Mountain National Forest Saco District Ranger Station: 33 Kancamagus Hwy; 603 447 5448; open daily

Mount Washington Cog Railway: Marshfield Base Station, off Rte 302; 603 278 5404; open Apr–Nov; adm

Conway Scenic Railroad: Rte 16, North Conway; 603 356 5251; Apr–Dec; adm

Pinkham Notch Visitor Center: Joe Dodge Lodge, Rte 16, north of North Conway; 603 466 2727; open daily

Whale's Tale Waterpark 481 Daniel Webster Hwy, Lincoln; 603 745 8810; open mid-Jun–Labor Day; adm

▪ In foliage season, drive the "Kanc" on a weekday, when there's less traffic.

5 Mount Washington Hotel and Resort

Legendary golfing and winter skiing are just two of the draws of this palatial, old-time White Mountain resort (above), which opened in 1902 (see p148).

Map of the White Mountains

9 North Conway

Gateway to the east side of the White Mountains, North Conway is a bustling commercial center. Spend the morning hiking, and the afternoon cruising for discounted designer goods at more than 200 outlet stores.

10 Whale's Tale Waterpark

With water slides for every age group, wave pools, wading pools, and a river that snakes through the 17-acre (7-ha) park, Whale's Tale is New Hampshire's top aquatic attraction.

6 Ski Mountains

Sudden drops and heavy snowfall make the White Mountains a top ski destination. Cannon Mountain (see p56) and Wildcat Mountain have lots of summer activities. Loon Mountain has great mountain-biking trails.

7 Pinkham Notch

This rocky pass is a hub for backcountry skiers and hikers. Hikes range from easy walking to challenging trails in Tuckerman Ravine.

8 Lincoln and Woodstock

With the Kancamagus Highway to the east and Franconia Notch to the north, Lincoln and Woodstock (below) are the civilized little villages that serve as easy-going base camps for hikers, climbers, skiers, and other outdoors enthusiasts.

Following pages Acorn Street in Beacon Hill, Boston

TOP 10 ★ Litchfield Hills, Connecticut

Tucked into the northwest corner of Connecticut, the undulating Litchfield Hills are the most scenic and bucolic section of the state. Technically an extension of the Taconic Mountains and the Berkshire Hills, the region is laced with a network of mountain streams, making fly-fishing for trout a leading springtime activity. Most sizable towns nestle in the valley of the Housatonic River, and their historic homes attest to Colonial settlement and recent gentrification by wealthy New Yorkers.

1 Mount Tom State Park

Views from the summit of Mount Tom entice hikers to this modest peak – an elevation gain of only 500 ft (152 m). The park's lake is a favorite with families and scuba divers alike.

4 Kent Falls State Park

North of the village of Kent, this park is home to an impressive water-fall **(right)**, a 250-ft (76-m) drop over slate and marble. Follow the trail to the top to see the most vigorous chute of all.

6 Litchfield

Local gentry flock to this market town to shop, dine, worship, and admire the many historic homes, including the first US law school (1784).

2 Lake Waramaug

Farmland around New Preston's Lake Waramaug **(above)** is temperate enough to grow wine grapes. Stop by Hopkins Vineyard to sample the wines. A state park on the broad, scenic lake offers picnic grounds, swimming and fishing.

3 Farmington River Tubing

Chill out on a summer day by floating down the Farmington River on an inflatable tube. The 2.5-mile (4-km) course takes in gentle ripples, a segment of turbulent rapids, and a lot of idle floating.

5 Lime Rock Park

Stock cars, road racers, and formula vehicles speed around the 1.5-mile (2.4-km) race track at Lime Rock Park. Highspeed driving classes are also offered here.

Map of Litchfield Hills

⑧ Shepaug Dam

In icy winter, more bald eagles **(left)** congregate at the Shepaug Dam in Southbury than almost any other place in New England. Camouflaged blinds let bird-watchers get close-up views.

⑦ Housatonic River

As the Housatonic River approaches the covered bridge at West Cornwall, it enters a 12-mile (19-km) stretch that many rank the best fly-fishing in the eastern US. Join sportspeople from New England trying their luck here in the spring.

⑨ Institute for American Indian Studies

Tucked high into the hilly woods of Washington, this facility re-creates a pre-European-contact Algonkian village. With a collection of artifacts dating back 10,000 years, it's the perfect spot to learn about the wood-lands culture of north-western Connecticut.

⑩ Woodbury

Join collectors and interior decorators as they scour Woodbury's 40-plus antiques dealers. In the village center, check out late-18th-century style *(see p98)* at the historic Glebe House Museum **(left)**.

NEIGHBORS WITH NAMES

The combination of Litchfield Hills' rural beauty and the easy proximity to New York City conspire to make it the home of many celebrities. Among the residents over the years have been sculptor Alexander Calder, chef Jacques Pepin, author William Styron, and a number of actors, including Meryl Streep.

NEED TO KNOW

MAP B4–5

Mount Tom State Park: Rte 202, Litchfield; 860 567 8870; open daily; adm

Farmington River Tubing: 92 Main St, New Hartford; 860 693 6465; open late May–early Sep; adm

Kent Falls State Park: Rte 7, Kent; 860 927 3238; open daily; adm

Lime Rock Park: 60 White Hollow Rd, Lakeville; 860 435 5000; open Apr–Oct; adm

Shepaug Dam Bald Eagle Observation Area: River Rd, Southbury; 800 368 8954; open late Dec–mid-Mar; bookings are required

Institute for American Indian Studies: 38 Curtis Rd, Washington; 860 868 0518; open Wed–Sun; adm

....

▨ Visit the gardens of White Flower Farm (167 Litchfield Rd, Morris; 860 567 8789) on Rte 63 south of Litchfield.

▨ Eat barbecued meats at The Cookhouse in New Milford *(see p101)*.

🔟⭐ Green Mountains, Vermont

The backbone of Vermont, these mountains run north-south from Quebec to the Massachusetts border, between the Champlain and Connecticut River valleys. Much of this stunning wilderness is set aside as the Green Mountain National Forest, which draws millions of visitors in every season for fishing, hiking, canoeing, mountain biking, camping, skiing, and snowshoeing. State Route 100, which runs between the east and west ranges of the Green Mountains, is among the most striking roads in the country for fall foliage.

① Stowe and Mount Mansfield

The Von Trapps of *Sound of Music* fame settled in Stowe **(above)** because it so resembled the Austrian Alps. Hikers and skiers flock to the village at the foot of Mount Mansfield.

② Killington

At 4,241 ft (1,292 m), Killington is the second-highest peak in these mountains (see p56) and home to the largest ski resort in eastern North America.

③ Middlebury

Prestigious Middlebury College adds sophistication to this typical New England community of Colonial homes and pointy-spired churches. Visit the old mill buildings along Otter Creek for a photogenic water-fall and shops.

④ Bennington

The Bennington Battle Monument **(left)** commemorates a major American Revolutionary War victory and provides sweeping panoramas of this southwest corner of the Green Mountains. The Bennington Museum (see p110) displays important folk art and Americana.

⑤ Hildene

This 24-room Georgian Revival house was built for Robert Todd Lincoln (1843–1926), the diplomat son of Abraham Lincoln (1809–65). Its highlights include family memorabilia and a 1,000-pipe Aeolian organ. Some 12 miles (19 km) of sur-rounding trails entice hikers, snowshoers, and cross-country skiers.

6 Mount Equinox Skyline Drive

This 5-mile (8-km) toll road **(above)**, along a high ridge, offers spectacular sunsets and breathtaking views of the Green, Adirondack, White, Berkshire, and Taconic mountain ranges.

7 Manchester

A genteel vacation resort since the 1890s, Manchester is so posh that its sidewalks are marble. Shop in the upscale designer outlet stores on the outskirts, or hit the slopes at nearby Stratton and Bromley ski areas.

8 Robert Frost Wayside

Poet Robert Frost (1874–1963) and the Vermont landscape where he farmed are inseparable. See nature through a poet's eyes by following the effortless interpretive trail in Ripton to a cabin where he wrote much of his later verse.

9 Mad River Valley

Tucked between two ranges of the Green Mountains, this region boasts a ski area *(see p57)*, chic Waitsfield village, and the outdoors sports center of Warren. Historic covered bridges cross many streams.

10 The Long Trail

This 270-mile (432-km) path follows the Green Mountains from Massachusetts to Quebec, crossing most of Vermont's highest peaks. Take a day hike between access points **(below)**.

Map of the Green Mountains

NEED TO KNOW

MAP K3–6, J6

Green Mountain National Forest Manchester Ranger Station: 2538 Depot St, Manchester Center; 802 362 2307; open Mon–Fri

Bennington Battle Monument: 15 Monument Circle, Bennington; 802 447 0550; open daily Apr–Oct; adm

Hildene: 1005 Hildene Rd, Manchester; 802 362 1788; open daily; adm

Green Mtn Club Visitor Center: 4711 Waterbury-Stowe Rd; 802 244 7037; open mid-May–mid-Oct: daily; mid-Oct–mid-May: Mon–Fri

■ Especially in the north, temperatures plummet in winter, spelling icy conditions. Be prepared for road closures.

■ The Warren Store (284 Main St, Warren) has hot grilled food, sandwiches, pastries, and sweets at breakfast and lunch.

TOP 10 ⭐ Portland and Casco Bay, Maine

The motto of Maine's largest city is *Resurgam*, or "I shall rise again," for good reason. Portland has burned down four times since its foundation in 1633. Building codes set up after the 1866 Great Fire created a legacy of handsome Victorian structures. Redevelopment has transformed the waterfront with dining and entertainment, and former warehouses have become boutiques and galleries. A short drive from downtown lie the parks and sandy beaches of Casco Bay.

1 Victoria Mansion
Portland-born hotelier Sylvester Morse (1816–93) made his fortune in New Orleans. The elaborate Italianate manse **(below)** he built in 1860 as his summer home showed the folks back home how well he'd done.

2 Two Lights State Park
Sandy dunes and rocky points meet at this state park, named for a pair of 19th-century lighthouses.

3 Windjammer and Whale-Watching Cruises
You might see humpback, finback, and minke whales roll in the water, spout, and leap during a 4-hour whale-watching trip, or view Portland from Casco Bay on a 2-hour sail aboard a gaff-rigged sloop.

4 Portland Head Light and Fort Williams Park
Maine's oldest lighthouse, Portland Head **(below)** was completed in 1791 as part of Fort Williams. This stately beacon marking the entrance to Casco Bay is one of the world's most photographed lighthouses.

5 Old Port District
The colorful shops of the Old Port District **(below)** range from dealers in antiques and fine crafts to coffee roasters, candy stores, and boutiques. Both fresh-caught lobsters and harbor island commuters come ashore at the docks.

6 Crescent Beach State Park
Spread out a blanket on the mile-long arc of beach, go exploring for shells, and take a dip to appreciate the soft sand and safe waters at this park, which is favored by Portland locals but little known to travelers.

Map of Portland and Casco Bay

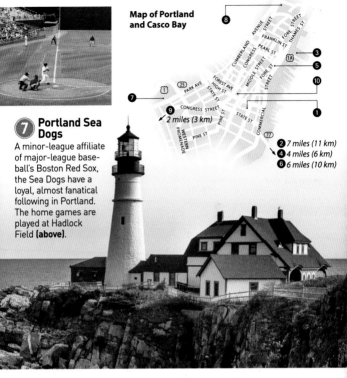

7 Portland Sea Dogs

A minor-league affiliate of major-league baseball's Boston Red Sox, the Sea Dogs have a loyal, almost fanatical following in Portland. The home games are played at Hadlock Field **(above)**.

8 Portland Observatory

Built in 1807 to alert merchants when their ships were arriving, this 86-ft (26-m) wooden observation tower is the last remaining US maritime signal station. It provides fine views of Portland harbor.

NEED TO KNOW

MAP N4

Two Lights State Park: Cape Elizabeth; 207 799 5871; adm

Odyssey Whale Watch: 170 Commercial St; 207 775 0727; adm

Maine Sailing Adventures: Maine State Pier, Commercial St; 207 749 9169; adm

Portland Head Light and Fort Williams Park: Shore Rd, Cape Elizabeth; 207 799 2661

Crescent Beach State Park: Rte 77, Cape Elizabeth; 207 799 5871; adm

Portland Sea Dogs: 271 Park Ave; 800 936 3647; adm

Portland Observatory: 138 Congress St; 207 774 5561; adm

Children's Museum and Theatre of Maine: 250 Thompson's Pt Rd; 207 828 1234; adm

■ Be prepared for steep walking; residential Portland is on a high ridge, downtown on a slope.

9 Children's Museum and Theatre of Maine

An ambitious program of plays for children and interactive exhibits that both entertain and enlighten make the Children's Museum and Theatre of Maine an essential place to visit with kids up to age 12.

10 Portland Museum of Art

Linking three new and historic buildings, the museum features painters of the Maine landscape, notably Winslow Homer (1836–1910), Marsden Hartley (1877–1943), and Rockwell Kent (1882–1971) *(see p40).*

🔟⭐ Lakes Region, New Hampshire

The stunning lakes dotting the high plateau and foothills south of the White Mountains began attracting settlers in the mid-18th century. Roads and railroads proliferated here in the 19th century, opening New Hampshire's lakes to tourism. There's something for everyone, from the strand of Weirs Beach to the stately grace of Wolfeboro; from the roaring racetrack in nearby Loudon to the tranquility of Squam Lake.

Lake Winni-pesaukee ①
At 21 miles (34 km) long, Winnipesaukee (**right**) is New Hampshire's largest lake. Swimmers from across the state love to congregate on its pine-clad beaches, while the more daring also race motorboats and hold waterskiing contests.

② Weirs Beach
Fun-lovers swarm this brassy resort (**below**) on the west end of Lake Winnipesaukee, where the beach and boardwalk are augmented by fair-ground rides, a water slide, mini-golf, souvenir shops, and all the cotton candy you can eat.

Map of the Lakes Region

Moultonborough ⑤ ⑥
Holderness ⑨
Meredith ⑧ Ossipee ⑯
④ Tuftonboro ①
② Weirs Beach ⑦
Lakeport Glendale Wolfeboro
Laconia ⑩
③

③ M/S Mount Washington
Cruising on this 230-ft (70-m) historic vessel is the most relaxing way to see Lake Winnipesaukee; while you relax, listen to a running commentary on celebrity homes and natural attractions along the way.

④ Winnipesaukee Scenic Railroad
You never lose sight of Winnipesaukee on summer shoreline excursions between Meredith and Lakeport, with stopovers at Weirs Beach. The railroad also operates weekend fall foliage over the mountains to Plymouth.

6 Castle in the Clouds

Tour this stone castle **(left)**, set on a bluff 750 ft (229 m) above Lake Winnipesaukee. Then hike some of the 28 miles (45 km) of trails, or take a stroll to a waterfall.

7 Wolfeboro

The village, a resort destination since 1763, when the Royal Governor built a summer home here, represents the demure, gentrified side of Winnipesaukee and is the largest community on the lake.

8 Meredith

Warm-water bass fishing is one of the lures of upscale Meredith, the epicenter of tasteful resort development on Lake Winnipesaukee. Capitalizing on New Hampshire's lack of sales tax, Meredith is also the lake's premier shopping destination.

MOTORCYCLE WEEK

Tens of thousands of motorcycle enthusiasts gather in and around Laconia in mid-June for the adrenaline-charged touring, partying, and races of the Laconia Motorcycle Week, a popular annual event since 1925. Area lodging books up in advance.

9 Ossipee

Enjoy hiking, blackberry picking, and horseback riding in quiet country roads around Ossipee, set in a pond-dotted plateau just east of Lake Winnipesaukee.

10 Gunstock Mountain Resort

Born as a Depression-era public works project, Gunstock has evolved into a popular ski area. In summer, vast forests make it a favorite for outdoor pursuits.

Squam Lake 5

Best known as the loon-haunted lake of the 1981 movie *On Golden Pond*, Squam **(right)** is a natural paradise, best appreciated on a boat tour with a guide from the Squam Lakes Natural Science Center.

NEED TO KNOW

MAP M4–5

Lakes Region Association: Exit 20, Tilton; 603 286 8008

M/S Mount Washington: 211 Lakeside Ave, Weirs Beach; 603 366 5531; open late May–mid-Oct; adm

Winnipesaukee Scenic Railroad: 154 Main St,

Meredith; 603 745 2135; open May–Oct; adm

Squam Lakes Natural Science Center: Rte 113, Holderness; 603 968 7194; open daily May–Oct; cruises May–Oct; adm

Castle in the Clouds: Moultonborough (Rte 171); 603 476 5900; open daily mid-May–mid-Oct; adm

Gunstock Mountain Resort: 719 Cherry Valley Rd, Gilford; 603 293 4341; open year-round; adm

■ Catch free concerts on selected summer evenings at Cate Park bandstand in Wolfeboro.

■ For dining with views of Winnipesaukee, try Patrick's Pub & Eatery (see p120).

TOP 10 ⭐ Berkshires, Massachusetts

Colonial-era villages of the southern Berkshires attest to the rich soils of the Housatonic Valley, while former brick mill towns of the north hint at 19th-century industrialization. Today, though, the region's identity revolves around the summer arts scene: music, dance, theater. The natural world, too, is always alluring. Mountain laurel explodes into bloom in June, and deer browse in abandoned apple orchards. Mountaintop trails lead to sweeping views, or you can hike into deep woods where a waterfall plunges into a still pool.

③ Mount Greylock

American authors Nathaniel Hawthorne and Henry David Thoreau climbed Greylock and sang its praises. You can reach the summit via scenic hiking trails or by taking the seasonal auto road.

① Williamstown

Williams College **(above)** lends a young spirit to this historic village at the edge of Mount Greylock. The Clark *(see p41)* holds several unmissable treasures.

② Norman Rockwell Museum

The museum **(left)** focuses on illustrator Normal Rockwell (1894–1978), whose works celebrate small-town American life in the mid-20th century. Other exhibitions explore the work of modern illustrators.

Map of the Berkshires

NEED TO KNOW

MAP B2–3

Berkshires Visitors Bureau: 66 Allen St, Pittsfield; 413 499 1600; open Mon–Fri

Norman Rockwell Museum: 9 Rte 183, Stockbridge; 413 298 4100; open Thu–Tue year-round; adm

Mount Greylock State Reservation Visitor Center: 30 Rockwell Rd, Lanesborough; 413 499 4262; open daily year-round

■ If you're looking for an easy climb, try modest Monument Mountain on Rte 7 a few miles south of Stockbridge. The roundtrip hike to the summit takes about 90 minutes.

■ Head to the deli behind Rubiner's Cheesemongers (264 Main St, Great Barrington; 413 528 0488) for gourmet sandwiches, many with exotic cheeses.

7 Jacob's Pillow Dance Festival

This woodsy mountaintop retreat in Becket is the venue for performances by top-flight dance companies from around the world (see p81), as well as workshop productions of edgy new choreography.

8 North Adams

This erstwhile factory town at the west end of the Mohawk Trail has embraced the art world and vice versa. It is best known for Mass MoCA (see p40), where provocative contemporary art fills a former factory.

9 Hancock Shaker Village

Now a museum and a working farm, Hancock was among the most influential communities of the celibate religious sect of Shakers (see p39). Its Round Stone Barn is considered to be a masterpiece of vernacular architecture.

4 Stockbridge

American illustrator Norman Rockwell (1894–1978) modeled his nostalgic treatments of rural American life on the people and buildings of this slow-paced village (above), dominated by the Red Lion Inn.

5 Lenox

A quaint village surrounded by grand houses and vast estates largely built as summer "cottages" between 1880 and 1910, Lenox is the epicenter of luxury shopping and the summer performing arts scene.

6 Great Barrington

A vibrant mix of artists, artisans, savvy business folk, and New Age visionaries makes Great Barrington easily the hippest town in the Berkshires, as well as a gateway to antiques shopping on Route 7 south of town.

10 Tanglewood Music Center

The summer home of the Boston Symphony Orchestra (below) since 1937, Tanglewood Music Center also hosts jazz, chamber music, and popular music concerts, and in summer operates an important music education program.

The Top 10 of Everything

Courtyard at Isabella Stewart Gardner Museum, Boston

TOP10 Moments in History

1 **10000 BC–AD 1000: Settlement**

As glaciers retreated from New England some 12,000 years ago, hunters moved in. By AD 1000, they lived in seasonal villages and farming augmented hunting and fishing. Most spoke an Algonkian language; their dialects persist on Native American lands in Massachusetts, Maine, and Connecticut.

2 **1620: Colonization**

Religious reformers from England swarmed into New England; first the Pilgrims at Plymouth, Massachusetts (1620), then Puritan colonies with Salem (1626) and Boston (1630). Soon communities were springing up in Rhode Island, Connecticut, and New Hampshire.

Painting depicting the Revolution

3 **1775: Revolution**

Tensions between mother country and colonies came to a head in 1775 with the occupation of Boston. On April 19, British redcoats and American rebels exchanged fire in Lexington and Concord. Within weeks, the American Revolution had begun.

A merchant vessel in Salem

4 **1785: Trade with China**

In 1785, merchants from Salem, Massachusetts, opened China to American trade. By 1845, shipbuilders in New England had developed the Yankee clipper, a swift sailing vessel that dominated the China trade well into the 1860s.

5 **1799–1821: Industrialization and Manufacturing**

From 1799 to 1813, Eli Whitney's Connecticut gun plants pioneered interchangeable parts and the assembly line. In 1821, textile entrepreneurs brought the Industrial Revolution to Lowell, Massachusetts, complete with purloined English loom designs and a factory-city scheme that was quickly replicated throughout the region.

6 **1820–60: Whaling Hegemony**

In the 1700s, Nantucket Islanders were among the first to hunt whales around the globe. The whale-oil business proved immensely lucrative, justifying larger ships and longer voyages. New Bedford, Massachusetts, was the world capital of whaling from the 1820s until the 1860s, when petroleum displaced whale oil.

7 **1861–5: Abolition and the Civil War**

New England led the fight to abolish slavery in the United States. The region harbored freedom seekers, and abolition societies flourished in both Black and white communities. New Englanders volunteered in overwhelming numbers to fight for the Union in the Civil War (1861–5), which decimated many rural areas.

⑧ 1865–1900: The Gilded Age

In the late 19th century, great wealth was generated as railroads spanned the country, industry expanded exponentially, and immigrants flowed into the country to fill job openings.

⑨ 1890–1950: The Rise of Tourism

Railroad construction opened the mountains and coasts of New England to scenic tourism. After World War II, new highways and roadside motels brought multitudes of new visitors to Cape Cod, the Maine coast, and the White and Green Mountains.

The Conway railroad, White Mountains

⑩ 1960–Today: Education and the Knowledge Economy

The founding of Harvard College in 1636 is what gave New England a head start in higher education. The emphasis on scholarship has persisted down the years, and has produced industrial leaders in such fields as information technology, robotics, and biotechnology.

TOP 10 REFORMERS AND REVOLUTIONARIES

US politician Bernie Sanders

1 Dorothea Dix (1802–87)
Advocate for the mentally ill, Dix also led Union Army nursing in the Civil War.

2 William Lloyd Garrison (1805–79)
Garrison edited the radical newspaper *The Liberator* and co-founded the American Anti-Slavery Society.

3 Joseph Smith (1805–44)
Vermont-born visionary Joseph Smith founded Mormonism.

4 Harriet Beecher Stowe (1811–96)
Prominent abolitionist Stowe attacked slavery in her famous 1852 novel, *Uncle Tom's Cabin*.

5 Clara Barton (1821–1912)
Nurse, teacher, and suffragist, Barton founded the US branch of the International Red Cross.

6 Mary Baker Eddy (1821–1910)
Eddy was the founder of the Christian Science movement.

7 Justice Oliver Wendell Holmes Jr. (1841–1935)
This Supreme Court Justice was noted for his blunt and pithy opinions.

8 W.E.B. DuBois (1868–1963)
A sociologist, scholar, and activist, DuBois was among the 20th century's most prominent civil rights leaders.

9 Rachel Carson (1907–64)
Marine biologist and writer, Carson rang the alarm on the use of pesticides in her seminal 1962 book, *Silent Spring*.

10 Bernie Sanders (b. 1941)
Progressive Vermont politician Sanders restored credibility to the American Left in his presidential nomination runs.

🔟 Colonial and Historic Sites

① Old Sturbridge Village, MA

MAP D3 ▪ Rte 20, Sturbridge ▪ 508 347 3362 ▪ Open mid-May–Nov: 9:30am–5pm Wed–Sun; call for winter hours ▪ Adm ▪ www.osv.org

Heritage livestock breeds and costumed guides create a vivid sense of New England rural life in the early 19th century at this living history museum. The village features more than 40 historic buildings moved from across the region.

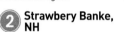

Minute Man statue

② Strawbery Banke, NH

MAP N6 ▪ 14 Hancock St, Portsmouth ▪ 603 433 1100 ▪ Open May–Oct: 10am–5pm daily; Call for off season tour hours ▪ Adm ▪ www.strawbery banke.org

Follow the development and growth of Portsmouth, NH, in this complex of historic dwellings assembled at Strawbery Banke, the city's original settlement. Period furnishings and historical gardens help to chronicle the daily life of the seaside city from 17th to 20th century.

③ Plimoth Patuxet, MA

MAP G3 ▪ 137 Warren Ave, Plymouth ▪ 508 746 1622 ▪ Open late Mar–Nov: 9am–5pm daily ▪ Adm ▪ www.plimoth.org

Step back in time to 1627 at Plimoth Patuxet's living history site. This engaging outdoor museum complex features a 17th-century English village, complete with costumed interpreters who narrate historical events, and Historic Patuxet, where visitors can discover more about the local Wampanoag culture.

④ Minute Man National Historical Park, MA

MAP E2 ▪ North Bridge Visitor Center: 174 Liberty St, Concord; 978 369 6993 ▪ Open daily (visitor center open Apr–Oct: 9:30am–5pm daily; call for winter hours) ▪ www.nps.gov/mima

On April 19, 1775, British troops engaged Colonial rebels in Lexington and Concord. This opening salvo of the American Revolution sent the British into retreat and galvanized other colonies to take up arms. Exhibits and annual reenactments depict a stirring historical moment.

⑤ Billings Farm & Museum, VT

MAP K5 ▪ 69 Old River Rd, Woodstock ▪ 802 457 2355 ▪ Open Apr–Oct: 10am–5pm daily; Nov–Feb: 10am–4pm Sat–Sun ▪ Adm ▪ www.billingsfarm.org

Set up in 1871, Billings Farm was turned into a museum of rural life in 1982. Its rolling green pastures and fine farm buildings represent the ideal of Vermont dairy farming. Visitors will get an opportunity to interact with sheep, horses, and chickens, and watch the herd of Jersey cows being milked.

English village in Plimoth Patuxet

6 Slater Mill, RI

MAP E4 ■ 67 Roosevelt
Ave, Pawtucket ■ 401 725 8638
■ Open Apr–Nov: 10am–4pm Wed–
Sun; tours 11am & 2pm (call ahead
to book) ■ www.nps.gov/blrv

Dating from 1793, Slater Mill
was the first successful cotton-
spinning mill in the United States.
The ingenuity of the early machinery,
which was driven by water power
transmitted through giant flapping
leather belts, will fascinate
engineering buffs.

Canterbury Shaker Village

7 Canterbury Shaker Village, NH

MAP M5 ■ 288 Shaker Rd, Canterbury
■ 603 783 9511 ■ Open May–Aug:
10am–4pm Tue–Sun; Sep–Oct:
10am–5pm daily; call for winter tour
hours ■ Adm ■ www.shakers.org

Founded in 1792, Canterbury was
a working Shaker village into the
1960s. Demonstrations and workshops teach you about
Shaker skills and ideals,
while informative daily
tours of original Shaker
buildings include fond
anecdotes of the sect's
final generation.

8 Weir Farm National Historic Site, CT

MAP B6 ■ 735 Nod Hill Rd,
Wilton ■ 203 834 1896
■ Open May–Oct: 10am–
4pm Wed–Sun; grounds
open dawn–dusk year-
round ■ www.nps.gov/wefa

The painter J. Alden
Weir (1852–1919) made

this rustic farm into a retreat for
himself and his friends at the end
of the 19th century. Two more
generations of artists worked here
before the property passed into the
care of the National Park Service.

9 Hancock Shaker Village, MA

MAP B2 ■ 1843 W. Housatonic St, Rte
20, Pittsfield ■ 413 443 0188 ■ Open
mid-Apr–late Jun: 10am–4pm daily;
late Jun–Oct: 10am–5pm daily ■ Adm
■ www.hancockshakervillage.org

Learn about the artful skills of the
Shakers at this settlement founded
in 1790. The iconic 1826 Round Stone
Barn perfectly encapsulates their
ability for making things both
functional and beautiful.

10 Lowell National Historical Park, MA

MAP F2 ■ Visitor Center: 246 Market
St, Lowell; 978 970 5000 ■ Open Jun–
Nov: 9am–5pm daily; call for off
season tour hours ■ Adm
■ www.nps.gov/lowe

Lowell launched the Industrial
Revolution in the United States, and
this urban park preserves the city's
network of canals and many of its
19th-century textile mills. The racket
of the mighty water-powered looms
operating in the 1864 Boott Cotton
Mill gives a real sense of what it
was like to work here.

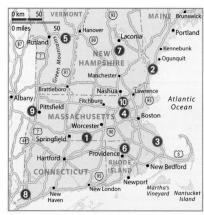

🔟 Art Museums

Isabella Stewart Gardner Museum

painters, including Marsden Hartley and Fitz Henry Lane. Tours of the Winslow Homer studio on Prouts Neck are also available from April through October.

4 Worcester Art Museum, MA

MAP E3 ▪ 55 Salisbury St ▪ 508 799 4406 ▪ Open 10am–4pm Wed–Sun ▪ Adm ▪ www.worcesterart.org
Striking Roman mosaics, arms and armor, and a top collection of pre-Columbian art from Mexico and Central America are the highlights at this general art museum.

1 Isabella Stewart Gardner Museum, Boston, MA

MAP S6 ▪ 25 Evans Way ▪ 617 566 1401 ▪ Open 11am–5pm Wed, Fri–Mon, 11am–9pm Thu ▪ Adm ▪ www.gardnermuseum.org
One of the all-time great private collectors, Gardner built this lovely Renaissance-style palace to display her 2,500-object collection.

5 Currier Museum of Art, Manchester, NH

MAP M6 ▪ 150 Ash St ▪ 603 669 6144 ▪ Open 11am–5pm Sun–Mon, Wed–Fri, 10am–5pm Sat ▪ Adm ▪ www.currier.org
In addition to its emphasis on 19th-century painting, the Currier Museum's collection embraces dynamic contemporary art as well.

2 Mass MoCA, North Adams, MA

MAP B2 ▪ 1040 Mass MoCA Way ▪ 413 662 2111 ▪ Open late Jun–Labor Day: 10am–6pm daily; Sep–late Jun: 11am–5pm Wed–Mon ▪ Adm ▪ www.massmoca.org
The Mass MoCA museum focuses on new work by living artists, and also stages dance, avant-garde theater, and performance art.

6 Museum of Fine Arts, Boston, MA

MAP S6 ▪ 465 Huntington Ave ▪ 617 267 9300 ▪ Open 10am–5pm Mon–Tue, Sat–Sun, 10am–10pm Wed–Fri ▪ Adm ▪ www.mfa.org
Highlights at Boston's world-class Museum of Fine Arts (MFA) include major holdings of Asian, Egyptian, and Nubian art. It also has the most important Monet collection outside of Paris.

3 Portland Museum of Art, Portland, ME

MAP N4 ▪ 7 Congress Sq ▪ 207 775 6148 ▪ Open 11am–6pm daily (to 8pm Fri) ▪ Closed mid-Oct–mid-May: Mon & Tue ▪ Adm ▪ www.portlandmuseum.org
Maine's largest art museum excels in major American landscape

Homer's *The Blue Boat* at Boston's MFA

7 Peabody Essex Museum, Salem, MA

MAP F2 ▪ East India Sq ▪ 978 745 9500 ▪ Open 10am–5pm Tue–Sun ▪ Adm ▪ www.pem.org
Staggering collections of China Trade treasures, furniture, and Asian art and artifacts fill this soaring building.

8 The Clark, Williamstown, MA

MAP B2 ▪ 225 South St ▪ 413 458 2303 ▪ Open Jul–Aug: 10am–5pm daily; Sep–Jun: 10am–5pm Tue–Sun ▪ Adm ▪ www.clarkart.edu
French Impressionists and English landscape artists are at the core of this diversified collection.

Avery Court, Wadsworth Atheneum

9 Wadsworth Atheneum, Hartford, CT

MAP C4 ▪ 600 Main St ▪ 860 278 2670 ▪ Open 11am–5pm Wed–Fri, 10am–5pm Sat–Sun ▪ Adm ▪ www.thewadsworth.org
America's oldest public art museum has New England's best collection of the startlingly oversized landscapes of the Hudson River School.

10 Shelburne Museum, VT

MAP J3 ▪ Rte 7, Shelburne ▪ 802 985 3346 ▪ Open May–mid-Oct: 10am–4pm daily; call for winter hours ▪ Adm ▪ www.shelburne museum.org
From elaborately stitched quilts to two elaborate miniature circuses, the museum celebrates American folk art and ingenuity.

TOP 10 ARTISTS OF NEW ENGLAND

Sculptor Louise Nevelson

1 John Singleton Copley (1738–1815)
America's first great portraitist, Bostonian Copley fled to England during the Revolution.

2 Fitz Henry Lane (1805–65)
Gloucester-based Lane revolutionized the handling of light in seascapes.

3 Winslow Homer (1836–1910)
Homer is most celebrated for his vigorous Maine seascapes.

4 Childe Hassam (1859–1935)
Hassam painted the streets of Boston and the Connecticut landscape with equal flourish.

5 Marsden Hartley (1877–1943)
Hartley painted powerful abstract landscapes of his native Maine.

6 Edward Hopper (1882–1967)
While spending his summers on the coast, Hopper painted scenes full of psychological nuance.

7 Louise Nevelson (1899–1988)
Raised in Maine, Nevelson is known for her monumental Abstract Expressionist sculptural assemblages.

8 Corita Kent (1918–86)
A former nun and graphic artist, Kent put social justice at the forefront of her Pop Art. Her *Rainbow Gas Tank* is a Boston landmark.

9 John Woodrow Wilson (1922–2015)
Lithographer, sculptor, and painter, Boston-born Wilson was known for his racially and politically charged art.

10 Molly Neptune Parker (1939–2020)
Neptune is famous for reviving and advancing the traditional art of Passamaquoddy basketry.

🔟 University Museums

1 Smith College Museum of Art, Northampton, MA

MAP C3 ■ 20 Elm St ■ 413 585 2760 ■ Open 11am–4pm Tue–Sun ■ Adm ■ www.scma.smith.edu

Since its founding in the 1870s, Smith has collected contemporary art. Rufino Tamayo's *Nature and the Artist: The Work of Art and the Observer*, commissioned by the college in 1943, offers a rare chance to see a work by one of Mexico's leading muralists.

2 Yale University Art Museums, New Haven, CT

MAP C5 ■ Yale Center for British Art: 1080 Chapel St; 203 432 2800; open 10am–5pm Tue–Sat, noon–5pm Sun; britishart.yale.edu ■ Yale University Art Gallery: 1111 Chapel St; 203 432 0600; open 10am–5pm Tue–Fri, 11am–5pm Sat–Sun; artgallery.yale.edu

The largest collection of British art outside the UK is kept at the Yale Center for British Art, designed by modernist architect Louis B. Kahn (1901–74). The Yale University Art Gallery, an earlier Kahn building of 1953, is noted for its American paintings and decorative arts.

3 Harvard Art Museums, Cambridge, MA

MAP F2 ■ 32 Quincy St ■ 617 495 9400 ■ Open 10am–5pm daily ■ Adm ■ www.harvardartmuseums.org

One of the world's most wide-ranging university art museums, this boasts outstanding collections of ancient Greek, medieval, Renaissance, Impressionist, Expressionist, and Asian art.

Exhibit, Harvard Art Museums

4 Colby College Museum of Art, Waterville, ME

MAP P3 ■ 5600 Mayflower Hill Dr ■ 207 859 5600 ■ Open 10am–5pm Tue–Sat, noon–5pm Sun ■ www.colby.edu/museum

An excellent survey of major American artists is capped with key holdings of modern and contemporary artists associated with Maine, including Marsden Hartley (1877–1943) and Alex Katz (b. 1927).

5 Peary-MacMillan Arctic Museum, Brunswick, ME

MAP P4 ■ Hubbard Hall, Bowdoin College ■ 207 725 3416 ■ Open 10am–5pm Tue–Sat, 2–5pm Sun ■ www.bowdoin.edu/arctic-museum

Named for Bowdoin College alumni Robert E. Peary (1856–1920) and Donald B. MacMillan (1874–1970), this museum brings their daring Arctic explorations to life. Natural history specimens, Inuit artifacts, and photographs offer insight on the cultures of the far north.

6 RISD Museum, Providence, RI

MAP E4 ■ 224 Benefit St ■ 401 454 6500 ■ Open 10am–5pm Wed, Sat & Sun, noon–7pm Thu & Fri ■ Adm ■ www.risdmuseum.org

Students at New England's top art and design school seek inspiration here. The historically

Yale Center for British Art

Manet's *Le Repos*, RISD Museum

encyclopedic collection of more than 100,000 objects is notable for late-19th-century painting (including French Impressionism), as well as post-1960 arts in various media. Contemporary studio crafts and furniture are also strong. Early American furniture stars in the decorative arts wing.

7 Hood Museum of Art, Hanover, NH

MAP L4 ■ Dartmouth College ■ 603 646 2808 ■ Open 11am–5pm Wed, Sat & Sun (to 8pm Thu & Fri) ■ hoodmuseum.dartmouth.edu

An ambitious expansion project has added new gallery space to showcase the 65,000-object collection. Highlights include Assyrian stone reliefs. Selections of Asian, sub-Saharan, and Native American art provide a global perspective.

8 Ballard Institute and Museum of Puppetry, Storrs, CT

MAP D4 ■ 1 Royce Circle, Suite 101B, University of Connecticut ■ 860 486 8580 ■ Call ahead for opening hours ■ Donation ■ www.bimp.uconn.edu

The key exhibits at this unique puppetry museum, one of America's largest, are the puppets of Frank

Ballard (1929–2010), a drama professor who set up America's first degree course in puppetry.

9 Harvard Museum of Natural History, Cambridge, MA

MAP F2 ■ 26 Oxford St ■ 617 495 3045 ■ Open 9am–5pm daily ■ Adm ■ www.hmnh.harvard.edu

This museum combines the charm of old-fashioned artifacts with cutting-edge science. The Glass Flowers exhibit is famous worldwide for its realistic re-creation of plants and blossoms. Dinosaur skeletons, gemstones, and meteorites are particularly popular with children.

10 Hudson Museum at University of Maine, Orono, ME

2 Flagstaff Rd ■ 207 581 1904 ■ Open 10am–3pm Mon–Fri ■ umaine.edu/hudson

This fascinating museum has a dedicated secton for ethnographic and archaeological Native American artifacts. The Penobscot basketry collection is the museum's prize display and ranks among the best in the world. Periodic workshops and exhibitions are held by leading Native American artists.

🔟 Personal Museums

1 John F. Kennedy Presidential Library and Museum, Boston, MA

MAP F3 ■ Columbia Point ■ 617 514 1600 ■ Open 9am–5pm daily ■ Adm ■ www.jfklibrary.org

This museum not only chronicles JFK's 1,000 days in office, it also touches on the man behind the myth.

John F. Kennedy Library and Museum

2 Orchard House, Concord, MA

MAP E2 ■ 399 Lexington Rd ■ 978 369 4118 ■ Open Apr–Oct: 10am–4:30pm Mon–Sat, 11am–4:30pm Sun; Nov–Mar: 11am–3pm Mon–Fri, 10am–4:30pm Sat, 1–4:30pm Sun ■ Adm ■ www.louisamayalcott.org

Louisa May Alcott (1832–88) not only set her 1868 classic *Little Women* in Orchard House, she also wrote it here.

3 Longfellow House–Washington's Headquarters National Historic Site, Cambridge, MA

MAP F2 ■ 105 Brattle St ■ 617 876 4491 ■ Open late-May–Oct: 9:30am–5pm Wed–Sun ■ www.nps.gov/long

The home of poet Henry Wadsworth Longfellow (1807–82), one of America's influential literary figures, lays bare both his triumphs and tragedies, such as the fire that killed his wife and scarred his face, making him grow his signature beard.

4 Saint-Gaudens National Historic Site, Cornish, NH

MAP L5 ■ Rte 12A ■ 603 675 2175 ■ Open late May–Oct: 9am–4:30pm daily; grounds open all year ■ Adm ■ www.nps.gov/saga

This house museum evokes the rustic idyll of the art colony that grew up around Augustus Saint-Gaudens (1848–1907), who was America's leading sculptor of the Beaux-Arts generation.

5 Robert Frost Farm, Derry, NH

MAP M6 ■ 122 Rockingham Rd ■ 603 432 3091 ■ Open May–mid-Oct: 10am–4pm Wed–Sun (Jun–Aug daily) ■ Adm ■ www.robertfrostfarm.org

Young poet Robert Frost found his voice while living here from 1900 to 1911, and began writing the verse set in the New England countryside that would win him four Pulitzer Prizes and the admiration of a nation.

6 The Mount, Lenox, MA

MAP B3 ■ 2 Plunkett St ■ 413 551 5111 ■ Open early May–Oct: 10am–5pm daily ■ Adm ■ www.edithwharton.org

This beautiful Berkshires estate in the gracious village of Lenox dates from 1902 and showcases the design and decorating sensibilities of literary giant Edith Wharton.

Wharton's boudoir at The Mount

7 Chesterwood, Stockbridge, MA

MAP B3 ■ 4 Williamsville Rd
■ 413 298 3579 ■ Open late May–
mid-Oct: 10am–5pm daily ■ Adm
■ www.chesterwood.org

The home and studio of Daniel
Chester French (1850–1931) vividly
recalls the sculptor best known
for his seated Abraham Lincoln in
Washington, D.C.'s Lincoln Memorial.

8 Mark Twain House, Hartford, CT

MAP C4 ■ 351 Farmington Ave
■ 860 247 0998 ■ Open 10am–
4:30pm daily (Jan–Feb: closed Tue)
■ Adm ■ www.marktwainhouse.org

Tiffany interiors feature in the
home of the great storyteller.
The adjoining museum revolves
around Twain (1835–1910) and
his contemporaries.

Romance of Autumn at Farnsworth

9 Farnsworth Art Museum, Rockland, ME

MAP Q3 ■ 16 Museum St ■ 207 596
6457 ■ Open Jun–Oct: 10am–5pm daily;
Nov–Dec & Apr–May: 10am–5pm Tue–
Sun; Jan–Mar: 10am–4pm Wed–Sun
■ Adm ■ www.farnsworth museum.org

The art dynasty of N.C. (1882–1945),
Andrew (1917–2009), and James
Wyeth (b.1946) is celebrated here.

10 Gropius House, Lincoln, MA

MAP F2 ■ 68 Baker Bridge Rd ■ 781
259 8098 ■ Open 11am–4pm Thu–Sun
(Nov–Apr: Sat–Sun only) ■ Adm
■ www.historicnewengland.org

Explore the family residence of the
highly influential architect Walter
Gropius (1883–1969).

TOP 10 NEW ENGLAND BOOKS

Acclaimed novelist John Irving

1 Hotel New Hampshire by John Irving
Comic turns abound in this literary
novel of despair and redemption at
an old resort hotel.

2 Country of the Pointed Firs by Sarah Orne Jewett
Revolutionary psychological novel
about women in rural coastal Maine,
first published 1896.

3 Outermost House by Henry Beston
Account of a year living on Cape
Cod's Great Beach.

4 American Primitive by Mary Oliver
This Pulitzer Prize-winning collection
by the celebrated LGBTQ+ poet covers
love and nature on Cape Cod.

5 Walden by Henry David Thoreau
Thoreau's philosophical musings in
the Massachusetts woods remain a
key text in American thought.

6 Mystic River by Dennis Lehane
Lehane's *noir* fiction reveals seamy
undercurrents of life on the edge
in South Boston.

7 Little Women by Louisa May Alcott
The four March girls struggle to
overcome character flaws.

8 Charlotte's Web by E. B. White
Children's classic fiction finds
philosophy in the barnyard.

9 The Wedding by Dorothy West
An intimate glimpse into African
American middle class life on
Martha's Vineyard in the 1950s.

10 Empire Falls by Richard Russo
Class-bound fatalism meets hope in
a dying mill town in Maine.

TOP 10 Maritime Sites

Skeleton, Nantucket Whaling Museum

1 Nantucket Whaling Museum, Nantucket, MA

MAP H5 ■ 13 Broad St ■ 508 228 1894 ■ Open late May–mid-Sep: 10am–5pm daily; call for winter hours ■ Adm ■ www.nha.org

Partially set in a former whale-oil refinery and candle factory, this museum tells how one small island dominated a lucrative industry for nearly a century. A 46-ft (14-m) sperm whale skeleton suspended from the ceiling sets the tone.

2 Mystic Seaport, CT

MAP D5 ■ 75 Greenmanville Ave, Mystic ■ 860 572 0711 ■ Open May–Oct: 10am–5pm daily; Nov–Dec: 10am–4pm Thu–Sun; call for winter hours ■ Adm ■ www.mysticseaport.org

Walk the decks of a tall ship, or see carpenters replank a vessel at this "museum of America and the sea." Mystic Seaport replicates a 19th-century coastal village with craftspeople plying their trades, historic vessels, and a working shipyard.

Tall ship, Mystic Seaport

3 New Bedford Whaling National Historical Park, New Bedford, MA

MAP F4 ■ 33 William St ■ 508 996 4095 ■ Open 10am–4pm Wed–Sun ■ Adm ■ www.nps.gov/nebe

In the 19th century, New Bedford was the world's leading whaling port. Many buildings of the era, including the Seamen's Bethel chapel mentioned in Herman Melville's *Moby-Dick*, have been preserved at this park. Don't miss the extraordinary scrimshaw carvings and a half-scale whaling ship at the New Bedford Whaling Museum.

4 Penobscot Marine Museum, Searsport, ME

MAP Q3 ■ 40 E Main St ■ 207 548 2529 ■ Open late May–mid-Oct: 10am–5pm Mon–Sat, noon–5pm Sun ■ Adm ■ www.penobscotmarinemuseum.org

Tiny Searsport was home to 10 per cent of America's deep-water sea captains by the close of the 19th century. Recapture the adventure of that time with captains' chests from the China Trade, a whale's jaw, and a wall of portraits of some 300 Searsport sea captains.

5 Maine Maritime Museum, Bath, ME

MAP P4 ■ 243 Washington St ■ 207 443 1316 ■ Open 9:30am–5pm daily ■ Adm ■ www.mainemaritimemuseum.org

Ships have been built at the mouth of the Kennebec

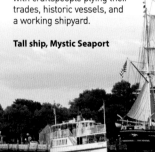

River for more than three centuries. At Maine Maritime Museum, sail-era artifacts, paintings of historic vessels, and displays of Maine maritime life chronicle both the practicalities and the romance of that trade.

6 Maine Lighthouse Museum, Rockland, ME

MAP Q3 ▪ 1 Park Dr ▪ 207 594 3301 ▪ Open Jun–Oct: 10am–4pm Wed–Mon; call for winter hours ▪ Adm ▪ www.maine lighthousemuseum.org

This is one of the world's largest collections of lighthouse artifacts. Marvel at gigantic prisms that made small lamps visible far out at sea, and learn how keepers lived.

7 Salem Maritime National Historic Site, Salem, MA

MAP F2 ▪ 2 New Liberty St ▪ 978 740 1650 ▪ Open May–Oct: 10am–5pm daily; Nov–Apr: 10am–4pm Wed–Sun ▪ www.nps.gov/sama

Salem's merchants brought the riches of the Far East back home. Uncover their fascinating story by retracing their steps along the historic wharves.

8 Historic Ship Nautilus and the Submarine Force Museum, Groton, CT

MAP D5 ▪ 1 Crystal Lake Rd ▪ 860 694 3174 ▪ Open May–Sep: 9am–5pm Wed–Mon; Oct–Apr: 9am–4pm Wed–Mon ▪ www.uss nautilus.org

Take a tour around the world's first nuclear-powered vessel and learn about the first submarine

Gold coin excavated by Expedition Whydah

to dive 20,000 leagues under the sea. Visitors can try commanding the sub at simulated controls.

9 Whydah Pirate Museum, W. Yarmouth, MA

MAP H4 ▪ 674 MA-28 ▪ 508 487 8899 ▪ Open 10am–5pm daily ▪ Adm ▪ www.discover pirates.com

"Black Sam" Bellamy went down with his ship in a storm off Cape Cod in April 1717. Popular with youngsters, this dockside display bristles with discoveries from the ongoing excavation of the wreck, including a hoard of authentic pirate treasure.

10 Lake Champlain Maritime Museum, Vergennes, VT

MAP J4 ▪ 4472 Basin Harbor Rd ▪ 802 475 2022 ▪ Open late May–mid-Oct: 10am–5pm daily ▪ Adm ▪ www.lcmm.org

Relics from the more than 200 ships that have been wrecked on Lake Champlain are displayed here. Full-size working replicas of historic vessels help to bring the lake's boating history alive.

🔟 Villages

1 Old Lyme, CT
MAP D5

If Old Lyme was not actually the cradle of American Impressionism, it was at least the art movement's summer camp from 1899 into the 1930s. Surprisingly little of either the landscape or the town has changed since that artistic heyday. Unlock the history with a visit to the Florence Griswold Museum (see p98), where many of the artists lodged.

2 Tiverton Four Corners, RI

The crossroads at the center of rural Tiverton on the east side of Narragansett Bay is filled with boutiques, antiques shops, and art galleries set in largely 18th-century buildings (see p88). The surrounding countryside is noted for its handsome historical stone walls and pastoral landscapes. The town also has arts and crafts galleries, an outstanding ice-cream stand, and a gourmet shop featuring local products.

3 Grafton, VT

This genteel village bunched around a 200-year-old tavern epitomizes rustic Vermont charm. Grafton Village Cheese Company makes top Vermont cheddars (see p108).

Entrance to the old tavern, Grafton

Colonial architecture, Wethersfield

4 Wethersfield, CT
Webb-Deane-Stevens Museum: 211 Main St, Wethersfield, CT; 860 529 0612; open May–Oct; adm; www.webb-deane-stevens.org

Founded in 1634 as one of the three original settlements in Connecticut, Wethersfield (see p95) remains an enclave of some of the most striking Colonial structures in the country – although architecture buffs can get equally excited about the distinctive early 20th-century Hubbard Bungalows. A visit to the three 18th-century homes of the Webb-Deane-Stevens Museum provides visitors with an interesting insight into the roots of the Colonial Revival movement in American style.

5 Wiscasset, ME
Nickels-Sortwell House: 121 Main St, Wiscasset, ME; 207 882 7169; open Jun–mid-Oct; adm; www.historicnewengland.org

A thriving shipbuilding town in the 18th and 19th centuries, Wiscasset immodestly claims to be the "prettiest village in Maine" (see p124). With baronial sea captains' homes that define the Federal style, a charming waterfront, and a generous sprinkling of boutiques and restaurants, it just might be. The 1807 Nickels-Sortwell House, built for a wealthy ship owner, recaptures Wiscasset's glorious past.

6 New London, NH
MAP L5

Without the overhead power lines and asphalt on the roads, New London would look as if time had stopped around 1850. Home to Colby-Sawyer College, a prestigious liberal arts school, New London bustles during the summer as the shopping and dining center for Lake Sunapee vacationers; another draw is the Barn Playhouse's summer stock theater season.

7 Kingfield, ME
MAP N2 ■ Stanley Museum: 40 School St, Kingfield, ME; 207 265 2729; open Mar–Dec; adm; www.stanleymuseum.org

Gateway to the Sugarloaf ski resort *(see p57)*, this characterful mountain village is a favorite with outdoors enthusiasts. The Stanley Museum chronicles the achievements of twin native sons Francis Edgar and Freelan Oscar Stanley, best known for inventing the steam-powered Stanley Steamer cars. Their sister Chansonetta's documentary photographs capture rural life.

8 Harrisville, NH
MAP L6

This charming New England mill village has revived the production of yarn and textiles using water power. Picturesque structures include the 1838 general store, historic brick mills, and several wooden workers' cottages. It is the only early 19th-century industrial community in New England still perfectly preserved in its original form. Keen knitters will want to visit the yarn factory and shop.

9 Watch Hill, RI

The gingerbread architecture of Westerly's seaside village of Watch Hill *(see p88)* reveals its Victorian roots – there's even a Victorian tea shop – but sport fishers come here for the perfect confluence of surf and shoreline currents.

10 Shelburne Falls, MA
MAP C2

Many artisans, musicians, and Sixties counterculture holdouts make their homes in this quirky village on the Mohawk Trail *(see p54)*. Cross the Deerfield River – which divides the town – on the Bridge of Flowers, a former railroad trestle heavily planted in blooms. The geological curiosity of glacial potholes scoured by a natural falls made the spot famous centuries ago.

Bridge of Flowers, Shelburne Falls

🔟 Islands

1 Monhegan Island, ME
Every seagull, twig, and moss-covered rock on Monhegan *(see p127)* must have been depicted in an artwork over the century or so since this fishing outpost off mid-coast Maine became a summer art colony. Once the summer folk have gone, the fishermen return.

A settlement on Monhegan Island

2 Nantucket Island, MA
MAP H5 ▪ Hyline Cruises: Ocean St Dock, Hyannis; 800 492 8082; www.hylinecruises.com
Thirty miles (48 km) off Cape Cod, Nantucket made its name through adventurous whaling and austere Quaker businessmen, who set the style with modest shingled homes. Pristine beaches, fascinating museums, and upscale shopping are among its present-day attractions.

3 Block Island, RI
Between Long Island and the Rhode Island coast, this tiny island looks like a tintype of a Victorian resort *(see p88)*. Its beaches, nature reserves, and historic lighthouses are best explored on a bike.

4 Isles of Shoals, NH
MAP N6 ▪ Portsmouth Harbor Cruises, Ceres St Dock; 603 436 8084; Jun–early Sep: Tue–Fri; adm; www.portsmouthharbor.com
These nine unforested rocky islands stand so far offshore that they were first used by English, Basque, and Breton fishermen as camps to dry their catch in the summer sun.

5 Mount Desert Island, ME
Shaped like a baseball mitt, this big island is home to the summer resort town of Bar Harbor *(see p14)* and the unspoiled paradise of Acadia National Park.

6 Isle au Haut, ME
MAP R4 ▪ Isle au Haut Boat Services: Seabreeze Ave, Stonington; 207 367 5193; www.isleauhaut.com
With primeval quaking bogs along the forested park trails and wild, wave-pounded bluffs, this craggy rock a few miles from Stonington offers the attractions of Mount Desert Island without the crowds.

7 Thimble Islands, CT
MAP C6 ▪ Thimble Island Cruise: Town Dock at Stony Creek; 203 488 8905; Jun–Oct; www.thimbleislandcruise.com
Stories and legends abound about the Thimble Islands, a cluster of diminutive islets located just off the coast. On a narrated scenic cruise you're very likely to hear a few of those tales, including the legend that the infamous pirate Captain Kidd buried treasure on Money Island. His gold hasn't been found to this day.

Islet, Thimble Islands

8 Boston Harbor Islands, MA

MAP F2 ■ 617 223 8666 ■ May–mid-Oct ■ www.bostonharborislands.org

The Boston Harbor Islands have sandy hiking and nature trails, lifeguard-protected beaches, and a few old forts. You can reach the islands by ferry from Boston's Long Wharf.

9 Martha's Vineyard, MA

MAP G5 ■ Steamship Authority: Woods Hole Terminal; 508 477 8600; steamshipauthority.com

Martha's Vineyard has something for everyone, from proper Edgartown and the gingerbread architecture of Oak Bluffs to the sacred multicolored clay cliffs revered by the Aquinnah Wampanoag community.

Oak Bluffs, Martha's Vineyard

10 Plum Island, MA

MAP F1 ■ Plum Island Turnpike, Newburyport; daylight hours; parking fee in summer; www.newburyport.com

This barrier island stretches 11 miles (18 km) south from Merrimack River and offers sandy beaches great for swimming. The island is a wildlife refuge and home to several bird habitats. Note that access is limited during plover nesting season.

TOP 10 LIGHTHOUSES

The Sheffield Island lighthouse

1 Sheffield Island
MAP B6 ■ Norwalk Harbor, CT
Handsome lighthouse built in 1868.

2 Stonington Harbor
MAP E5 ■ 7 Water St, Stonington, CT
Granite lighthouse, now a museum.

3 West Quoddy Head
MAP R2 ■ Quoddy Head State Park, Lubec, ME
This iconic candy-striped light (1857) marks the easternmost point of the US.

4 Marshall Point
MAP Q4 ■ Marshall Point Rd, Port Clyde, ME
Offshore light connected by a walkway to the keeper's house and museum.

5 Pemaquid Point
MAP P4 ■ Off Rte 130, Bristol, ME
Built high on dramatic ledges in 1835, Pemaquid Point remains an essential navigational aid.

6 Portsmouth Harbor
MAP N6 ■ Off Rte 1B, New Castle, NH
Built in 1878, this is the latest of several built on New Castle island since 1771.

7 Beavertail
MAP E5 ■ Beavertail State Park, Jamestown, RI
This is the third-oldest light on the eastern seaboard, built in 1783.

8 Highland
MAP H3 ■ N Truro, MA
Set atop a bluff at the Cape Cod National Seashore, this is the highest light on the New England mainland.

9 Nobska Point
MAP G5 ■ Falmouth, MA
Sitting on the Shining Sea Bike Path, Nobska is visible for 16 miles (26 km).

10 Great Point
MAP H5 ■ Nantucket Island, MA
Rebuilt in 1986 as a historic replica in the Coskata-Coatue Wildlife Refuge.

🔟 Ocean Beaches

Brightly colored structures on the pier at Old Orchard Beach

① Old Orchard Beach, Old Orchard, ME

Old Orchard has been a razzle-dazzle resort beach since trains first ran here in 1842. Three miles (5 km) of main beach guarantee plenty of room for sunbathing, swimming, kite-flying, and sandcastle-building. Shops, amusements, and rides ensure no one ever gets bored (see p126). During the summer there's a lively bar scene as well.

② Hampton Beach, Hampton, NH

MAP N6

Small, decorous state beaches dot Hampton's shoreline, but the main village beach is easily the most raucous, with outdoor concerts, sandcastle competitions, a flurry of summer activities, and a strip of souvenir shops and casual eateries. In summer the town is bilingual, reflecting its popularity with Quebec vacationers. Swimming is good, but the surf from offshore storms can make it challenging at times.

③ Crane Beach, Ipswich, MA

MAP G2 ▪ **Adm**

This 7-mile (11-km) stretch of copious white sand is one of New England's most picturesque swimming beaches. Pack binoculars; Crane is legendary for its diversity of bird species, although some nesting grounds may be off-limits between May and early August.

④ Misquamicut State Beach, Westerly, RI

MAP E5 ▪ **Adm**

Misquamicut (miss-KWAHM-i-cut) is one of New England's most popular family beaches, packing intense summer entertainment into a relatively short stretch of white sand. Most rides, amusement stands, and food kiosks open late June to August and some fall weekends, but the beach is accessible all year. Parking lots fill early on summer weekends.

5 Salty Brine State Beach, Narragansett, RI

MAP E5 ▪ Adm

With solar-powered, hot-water showers and electricity from wind turbines to supply the juice to recharge electric vehicles, this is the "greenest" beach facility in New England. The narrow strip of fine golden sand at the entrance to Galilee harbor has gentle waves, great views of fishing vessels, and some of the coast's finest seafood.

6 Coast Guard Beach, Eastham, MA

MAP H4 ▪ Adm

Arguably the best swimming beach on Cape Cod, Coast Guard Beach marks the beginning of the 30-mile (48 km) Great Beach of the Cape Cod National Seashore. A long and generous slope of sand leads down to the ocean, so the beach is rarely crowded. Stroll southward onto Nauset Spit to watch shore birds in summer, seals in winter.

7 Hammonasset Beach State Park, Madison, CT

MAP C5 ▪ Adm ▪ Camping late May–mid-Oct

More than 2 miles (3 km) of brown sand beaches lapped by the gentle waves of Long Island Sound lure summer swimmers and sunbathers in droves, but Connecticut's longest shorefront park also has an excellent nature center at Meigs Point. Fishermen stake out positions here early for excellent bluefish and striped bass fishing.

Vast sands at Hammonasset Beach

8 Old Silver Beach, Falmouth, MA

MAP G4 ▪ Adm

This beautiful beach overlooking Buzzards Bay has warm summer waters, low waves, and a very gradual drop-off, making it an ideal swimming spot for young kids. Half the beach is reserved for Falmouth residents; the other half is open to all. Facing west over Buzzards Bay, Old Silver has some of New England's most spectacular sunsets.

Reid State Park coastline

9 Reid State Park, Georgetown, ME

MAP P4 ▪ Adm

Reid State Park beaches are long strands of brown sand backed by high dunes – the antithesis of the "rocky coast of Maine." Mile Beach and Half Mile Beach have lifeguards, changing rooms, and snack bars in summer. You can swim safely along stretches sheltered from the ocean by sand bars, or break out the surf boards and head for more exposed parts of the beach.

10 Ogunquit Beach, Ogunquit, ME

MAP N5

A 2-mile (3-km) cove lined with brown sand, Ogunquit Beach is well served by a summer trolley system that makes parking a cinch. The south end of the beach terminates at romantic Marginal Way, a clifftop walking path through thickets of roses to the shops, restaurants, and copious art galleries of Perkins Cove.

🔟 Ways to See Foliage

1 Green Mountain Railroad, VT

MAP K5 ▪ 563 Depot St, Chester ▪ 800 707 3530 ▪ Open May–mid-Oct ▪ Adm ▪ www.rails-vt.com

Take a jaunt through the southern Vermont woods aboard vintage railcars, which are pulled by a diesel locomotive, for some spectacular views of the Connecticut River and the deep gorges of its tributaries. In fall, the maple trees are a dazzling blaze of flame-like colors.

2 Mohawk Trail, MA

This historic Native American trade route over the Berkshire Hills (see p80) follows the upper ranges of the Deerfield River – resplendent with acid-yellow alder and birch – until it climbs through fiery stands of maple, birch, and beech in the Charlemont State Forest. The drive ends by spiraling down the hillsides at the aptly named Hairpin Turn.

Colorful forests at Lake Champlain

3 Lake Champlain Cruise, VT

MAP J3 ▪ Burlington Boathouse, 1 College St, Burlington ▪ 802 862 8300 ▪ Open mid-May–mid-Oct ▪ Adm ▪ www.soea.com

Hop aboard the *Spirit of Ethan Allen III* for a narrated cruise around Lake Champlain. While adults admire the brightly painted forests that surround the lake, kids ought to keep an eye out for Champ, the legendary sea serpent that resides in the lake.

4 K-1 Gondola, VT

After a scenic gondola ride to the highest lift-served terrain in Vermont, a short, easy hike brings you to the summit of Killington Peak (see p56) for a panoramic view of five states and part of Canada.

Fall foliage, Kancamagus Highway

5 Kancamagus Highway, NH

Few foliage drives in New England match the thrill of hurtling along the "Kanc" through a tunnel of kaleidoscopic colors (see p20). This stretch of highway runs between Lincoln and Conway and covers about 34 miles (55 km) of Route 112. Stop along the way to savor the experience by hiking to a waterfall or sunning on midstream glacial boulders.

6 Essex Steam Train and Riverboat, CT

Combine a trip through the woods in restored 1920s railcars pulled by coal-fired steam locomotives with a cruise down the Connecticut River aboard a three-deck Mississippi-style riverboat (see p99).

7 Route 100, VT

MAP K2–6

Perhaps New England's ultimate road for leaf-peeping, Route 100 passes natural wonders like Moss Glen Falls, follows the Mad River through several scenic villages, then rises high into the Green Mountains.

8 Deerfield River Rafting, MA

MAP C2 ▪ Zoar Outdoor: 800 532 7483; open Apr–Oct; adm; www.zoaroutdoor.com

The Deerfield River has some of the most exhilarating rapids and most scenic gorges in New England. Nothing compares to the rush of bankside colors viewed from a raft during foliage season.

9 Boston's Emerald Necklace

MAP V4–W4 ▪ www.emeraldnecklace.org

Boston is blessed with an almost continuous chain of parks stretching from downtown skyscrapers to leafy suburbia. This walking and cycle route begins at Boston Common. In the fall, the parks are an explosion of red, purple, orange, and yellow.

10 Mount Monadnock, NH

MAP L6 ▪ Off Rte 124, west of Jaffrey ▪ 603 532 8862 ▪ Open sunrise–sunset daily ▪ Adm ▪ www.nhstateparks.org

The 3,165-ft (965-m) summit of Mount Monadnock offers incredible views. The scramble over boulders is worth the effort, especially during fall. Reservations recommended.

Hiker at Mount Monadnock

TOP 10 COVERED BRIDGES

Charming covered Stark Bridge

1 Stark Bridge, 1862
MAP M3 ▪ North Rd, Stark, NH
Paddleford truss spanning the Upper Ammonoosuc River in the village.

2 Cornish-Windsor Bridge, 1866
MAP L5 ▪ Rte 12A, Plainfield, NH
Town lattice, rebuilt in 1989. Spans the Connecticut River between New Hampshire and Vermont.

3 Hemlock Bridge, 1857
MAP M4 ▪ Off Rte 302, Fryeburg, ME
Paddleford truss over the Saco River.

4 Artist's Covered Bridge, 1872
MAP N3 ▪ Off Rtes 2 and 26, Newry, ME
Paddleford truss, also known as the Sunday River Bridge.

5 Bulls Bridge, 1842
MAP B4 ▪ Rte 7, Kent, CT
Town lattice and queenspost over the Housatonic River.

6 Albany Covered Bridge, 1858
MAP M4 ▪ Dugway Rd, off the Kancamagus Hwy, Albany, NH
Altered Paddleford truss across the Swift River.

7 Ashuelot Bridge, 1864
MAP K6 ▪ South of Rte 119, Bolton Rd, Upper Village, Winchester, NH
Town lattice truss that spans the Ashuelot River.

8 Warren Bridge, 1880
MAP K4 ▪ East of Rte 100, Warren, VT
Asymmetrical queenspost stretching across the Mad River.

9 Paper Mill, Silk, and Henry Bridges, 1840–2000
MAP J6 ▪ South of Rte 67A, Bennington, VT
Three bridges on the Waloomsac River.

10 Burkeville Bridge, 1870
MAP C2 ▪ Rte 116, Conway, MA
Howe truss bridge stretching across the South River.

🔟 Mountain Ski Areas

Skier on the slopes, Sunday River

1 Sunday River, Newry, ME

MAP M3 ▪ 15 South Ridge Rd ▪ 207 824 3000 ▪ Ski: mid-Nov–mid-Apr ▪ Adm ▪ www.sundayriver.com

The most accessible of Maine's high-mountain skiing, Sunday River splashes across eight interconnected peaks, with 135 diverse trails served by 18 lifts (including five high-speed quads). Lights extend evening skiing on most weekends and holidays. Snowmaking on 95 percent of terrain guarantees a long season. Evenings are enlived by the popular Shipyard Brew Haus microbrewery. During the summer it's a popular golf resort.

2 Bretton Woods, NH

MAP M3 ▪ 99 Ski Area Rd ▪ 603 378 3320 ▪ Ski: mid-Nov–Apr ▪ Adm ▪ www.brettonwoods.com

This is the largest ski area in New Hampshire boasting 464 acres (188 ha) of skiing and snowboarding on 63 trails, 35 glades, and three terrain parks. The ski area is closely allied with Omni Mount Washington Resort, so ski-stay packages give access to one of the last grand hotels of the White Mountains.

3 Killington, VT

MAP K5 ▪ 4763 Killington Rd ▪ 802 422 6200 ▪ Ski: mid-Nov–mid-Apr ▪ Adm ▪ www.killington.com

Killington Resort stretches across six mountain areas in central Vermont, providing 212 ski trails. As New England's largest ski resort, it also features 28 lifts, including three express gondolas and five express chairs, that give access to the highest lift-served ski terrain in the state of Vermont. Snowboarders' needs are also catered for with The Stash and Dream Maker terrain parks as well as the 500-ft (152-m) Superpipe with 22-ft (6.7-m) walls.

4 Mount Mansfield, Stowe, VT

MAP K3 ▪ 5781 Mountain Rd ▪ 802 253 3000 ▪ Ski: mid-Nov–mid-Apr ▪ Adm ▪ www.stowe.com

As the tallest of the attractive Green Mountains, Mansfield challenges hikers every summer and fall. Come winter, Stowe Mountain Resort takes over the slopes with 116 trails and more mile-long lifts than any other resort in the East. With average annual snowfall of 333 inches (8.46m), Stowe has a long season of deep snow. Summer golf resort.

5 Cannon Mountain, Franconia, NH

MAP L3 ▪ 9 Franconia Notch State Park ▪ 603 823 8800 ▪ Ski: Nov–mid-Apr ▪ Adm ▪ www.cannonmt.com

One of the oldest ski areas in the US, Cannon has a refreshingly noncommercial feel about it, not to mention the spectacular White Mountains vistas from its 97 trails.

Skiing at Cannon Mountain

6 Attitash, Bartlett, NH
MAP M4 ▪ Rte 302 ▪ 800 223 7669 ▪ Ski: late Nov–Apr ▪ Adm ▪ www.attitash.com

Not as big or challenging as some New England areas, Attitash (and attached Bear Peak) have vistas of the White Mountains to make the skiing memorable. The longest vertical drop is 1,750 ft (534 m), but 11 lifts serve 68 trails.

Ski lift going up Sugarloaf

7 Sugarloaf, Carrabasset Valley, ME
MAP N2 ▪ 5092 Sugarloaf Access Rd ▪ 207 237 2000 ▪ Ski: mid-Nov–late Apr ▪ Adm ▪ www.sugarloaf.com

Offering the only lift-served skiing above the treeline in the East, its 54 miles (87 km) of trails crisscross Sugarloaf, Maine's second-highest peak at 4,237 ft (1,291 m). The continuous vertical drop of 2,820 ft (860 m) is New England's longest. Sixty of Sugarloaf's 162 trails are rated difficult (black diamond) or expert (double black diamond). Summer golf resort.

8 Smugglers' Notch, Jeffersonville, VT
MAP K3 ▪ 4323 Rte 108 S ▪ 802 644 8851 ▪ Ski: mid-Nov–mid-Apr ▪ Adm ▪ www.smuggs.com

Smugglers' Notch, an all-season family resort, is well known for its learn-to-ski programs and activities for kids. The resort stretches across three peaks, with 8 lifts serving 78 trails. The skiing at Smugglers' can be challenging, despite its family orientation; the Black Hole is the only triple black diamond trail in the Eastern US. Visit during the summer and other attractions are offered as well, including fishing, waterparks, canoeing, and golf.

9 Mad River Glen, Waitsfield, VT
MAP K3 ▪ 802 496 3551 ▪ Ski: mid-Dec–early Apr ▪ Adm ▪ www.madriverglen.com

This mountain, with some of the East's most challenging terrain, is run by a co-op of hardcore skiers who keep it simple: no snowboards; a single-chair lift from 1948 that limits numbers on the slopes; and no fancy lodge or hotels with hot tubs.

10 Stratton Mountain, Stratton, VT
MAP K6 ▪ 5 Village Lodge Rd ▪ 802 297 4000 ▪ Ski: Nov–early May ▪ Adm ▪ www.stratton.com

A pioneer in snowboarding, this resort is located in the Green Mountain National Forest near Manchester, a town popular with both skiers and shoppers. The 11 lifts serving 99 trails and top-ranked terrain parks include four six-person chair lifts. Summer golf resort.

Following pages Covered bridge in Franconia, New Hampshire

🔟 Other Outdoor Activities and Sports

Hikers enjoying the scenery

1 Hiking
Appalachian Trail: www. outdoors.org ▪ Long Trail: www. greenmountainclub.org

Two US long-distance hiking trails cross New England. The Appalachian Trail begins in Georgia, crossing Vermont and New Hampshire before ending in Maine. The Long Trail traverses Vermont from south to north.

2 Cross-Country Skiing
Trapp Family Lodge: MAP K3; 700 Trapp Hill Rd, Stowe, VT; 802 253 8511; www.trappfamily.com ▪ Craftsbury Nordic Center: MAP K2; 535 Lost Nation Rd, Craftsbury Common, VT; 800 826 7000; open mid-Nov–Mar; adm; www.craftsbury.com

The epicenter of cross-country skiing is north-central Vermont. The von Trapp family (of *Sound of Music* fame) introduced Nordic skiing in Stowe. Craftsbury Nordic Center is home to legendary cross-country ski races.

3 Schooner Sails
MAP Q3 ▪ Rockland and Camden, ME ▪ 800 807 WIND (9463) ▪ Open Jun–Oct ▪ Adm ▪ www. sailmainecoast.com

Seals, porpoises, and whales are your neighbors as you sail where the winds take you with the schooners of Maine's windjammer fleet.

4 Bird-Watching
Wellfleet Bay: MAP H4; Rte 6, Wellfleet, MA; 508 349 2615; trails open 8am–dusk daily; adm; www. massaudubon.org ▪ Audubon: MAP A6; 613 Riversville Rd, Greenwich, CT; 203 869 5272; open dawn–dusk daily; adm; greenwich.audubon.org

Observe shore birds plus warblers and other migratory species at Wellfleet Bay Wildlife Sanctuary on Cape Cod. The Audubon Society in Greenwich, Connecticut, runs a convivial annual count.

5 Golf
Samoset: MAP Q3; 220 Warrenton St, Rockport, ME; 207 594 2511; open May–Nov; adm; www. samosetresort.com ▪ Ocean Edge: MAP H4; 2907 Main St, Brewster, MA; 508 896 9000; open Apr–Nov; adm; www.oceanedge.com

The most noted championship-level courses in New England include Samoset and Ocean Edge.

6 White-Water Rafting
MAP P1 ▪ West Forks, ME ▪ 800 723 8633 ▪ Open May–early Oct ▪ Adm ▪ www.raftmaine.com

White-water rafting is hugely popular in Maine. Many trips depart from The Forks, a hamlet on the Kennebec.

Rafting on the Penobscot River

7 Cycling
www.traillink.com

In Massachusetts, Minuteman Rail Trail cuts from Cambridge through Lexington and Concord. East Bay Bike Path is a tour of Narragansett Bay from Providence, Rhode Island. The Ashuelot Rail Trail from Keene to Hinsdale, New Hampshire, is a great way to explore covered bridges.

8 Whale-Watching
7 Seas: MAP G2; 63 Rogers St, Gloucester, MA; 978 283 1776; open late Apr–Oct; adm; www.7seas whalewatch.com

Large pods of whales summer on Stellwagen Bank. Take a cruise from Gloucester or Provincetown to look for finback, minke, and humpback whales, as well as dolphins.

Watching whales at Stellwagen Bank

9 Kayaking and Canoeing
Nauset: MAP H4; Goose Hummock Shops, Rte 6A, Orleans, MA; 508 255 0455; open May–Oct; adm; www.goosehummockshops.com ▪ Allagash: MAP N3; Mahoosuc Guide Service, 1513 Bear River Rd, Newry, ME; 207 824 2073; open May–Oct; adm; www.mahoosuc.com

Paddle among the wading birds of Nauset Marsh, or through Maine's pristine Allagash Wilderness.

10 Fishing
Orvis: MAP K6; 4180 Main St, Manchester, VT; 866 531 6213; www.orvis.com ▪ Frances Fleet: MAP E5; 33 State St, Narragansett, RI; 401 783 4988; adm; www.francesfleet.com

Orvis runs fly-fishing courses in Manchester, Vermont. Frances Fleet, operating out of Galilee, Rhode Island, offers deep-sea trips.

TOP 10 SPORTS TEAMS AND EVENTS

Ice hockey player, Boston Bruins

1 Boston Bruins
MAP W2 ▪ TD Garden, above North Station, Boston, MA ▪ Oct–Apr
One of the founding teams of the National Hockey League.

2 New England Patriots
MAP F3 ▪ Gillette Stadium, Foxborough, MA ▪ Sep–Jan
Perennial Super Bowl contenders.

3 Boston Celtics
MAP W2 ▪ TD Garden, above North Station, Boston, MA ▪ Oct–May
Hoop dreams ramp up each fall as the Celtics take the court.

4 Boston Red Sox
MAP S5 ▪ Fenway Park, Boston, MA ▪ Apr–Oct
The team plays in baseball's most hallowed park.

5 Head of the Charles Regatta
MAP F2 ▪ mid-Oct
The world's largest two-day rowing event between Cambridge and Boston.

6 Boston Marathon
MAP F2 ▪ mid-Apr
The world's oldest annual marathon, from Hopkinton to Boston.

7 New Hampshire Motor Speedway
MAP M5 ▪ Loudon, NH ▪ Apr–Oct
Sports cars, stock cars, and even go-karts thrill fans with their speed.

8 Newport Regatta
Topsail racing in the home of American yachting (see p19).

9 US National Toboggan Championships
MAP Q3 ▪ Camden, ME ▪ Feb
Camden Snow Bowl hosts annual open-entry tourney.

10 New England Revolution
MAP F3 ▪ Gillette Stadium, Foxborough, MA ▪ Mar–Oct
Boston's professional soccer team.

🔟 Children's Attractions

Riding a zipline, Ramblewild

① Ramblewild, Lanesborough, MA

MAP B2 ▪ 110 Brodie Mountain Rd ▪ 413 499 9914 ▪ Open Apr–Jun & Oct: 10am–1pm Wed–Sun; Jul–Sep: 9am–3pm daily (reservations recommended) ▪ Adm ▪ www.ramblewild.com

Eight trails of varying difficulty snake through the canopy with logs, nets, ziplines, rope bridges, and more.

② Boston Children's Museum

MAP X4 ▪ 308 Congress St ▪ 617 426 6500 ▪ Open 10am–5pm Sat–Thu (to 9pm Fri) ▪ Adm ▪ www.bostonkids.org

Hands-on learning fills two former wool warehouses. Children can scale a climbing sculpture, explore the magic of soap bubbles, or join in short plays and shows on KidStage.

③ Dinosaur State Park, Rocky Hill, CT

MAP C4 ▪ 400 West St ▪ 860 529 8423 ▪ Open 9am–4:30pm Tue–Sun ▪ Adm ▪ www.dinosaurstatepark.org

Children are awestruck by more than 500 dinosaur fossil tracks

preserved beneath a geodesic dome. Life-size dioramas re-create scenes from the Jurassic and Triassic eras.

④ McAuliffe-Shepard Discovery Center, Concord, NH

MAP M5 ▪ 2 Institute Dr ▪ 603 271 7827 ▪ Open mid-Jun–early Sep: 10:30am–4pm daily (call for winter hours) ▪ Adm ▪ www.starhop.com

Kids are encouraged to reach for the stars at this space exploration center named for astronauts Alan B. Shepard and Christa McAuliffe.

⑤ Six Flags New England, Agawam, MA

MAP C3 ▪ Rte 159 ▪ 413 786 9300 ▪ Open Apr–Oct, call for hours ▪ Adm ▪ www.sixflags.com

Some of the fastest, tallest, wildest, and most gut-wrenching thrill rides in the country await at this Six Flags amusement park located beside the Connecticut River.

⑥ Roger Williams Park and Zoo, Providence, RI

MAP E4 ▪ 1000 Elmwood Ave ▪ 401 785 3510 ▪ Hours vary, check website ▪ Adm ▪ www.rwpconservancy.org

Visitors can ride the carousel or enjoy a boat ride on the lake in this sprawling park, and visit the Museum of Natural History, the planetarium, and the Botanical Center. More than 100 species roam naturalistic settings in themed areas of the zoo.

Elephant, Roger Williams Zoo

Basketball Hall of Fame, Springfield, MA

MAP C3 ▪ 1000 Hall of Fame Ave ▪ 413 781 6500 or 877 4HOOPLA ▪ Open 10am–4:30pm daily ▪ Adm ▪ www.hoophall.com

This complex in the birthplace of basketball celebrates the sport with footage of games, star players' memorabilia, and interactive exhibits that are suitable for kids.

Lake Compounce, Bristol, CT

MAP C4 ▪ 185 Enterprise Dr ▪ 860 583 3300 ▪ Open May–Oct, call for schedule ▪ Adm ▪ www.lake compounce.com

A 1911 carousel, a 1927 roller coaster, and an antique trolley maintain the ambience of this amusement park. Most attractions, shows and restaurants are wheelchair accessible.

Penguins, New England Aquarium

New England Aquarium, Boston

MAP X3 ▪ Central Wharf ▪ 617 973 5200 ▪ Open Jun–early Sep: 9am–6pm Mon–Thu & Sat–Sun (10am–8pm Fri); early Sep–May: 10am–5pm Mon–Thu & Sat–Sun (10am–8pm Fri) ▪ Adm ▪ www.neaq.org

Kids love the acrobatics of the harbor seals, the antics of more than 80 penguins, and the shark and ray tank.

Ben & Jerry's Ice Cream Factory, Waterbury, VT

The factory tour of Ben & Jerry's (*see p111*) is a real hoot. The goal is the tasting room at the end, where you might sample flavors in development.

TOP 10 CAROUSELS

The carousel at Bushnell Park

1 Flying Horse Carousel
MAP E5 ▪ Bay St, Watch Hill, RI ▪ Adm
Beachfront carousel that is one of the oldest in New England.

2 Heritage Museums & Gardens
MAP G4 ▪ 67 Grove St, Sandwich, MA ▪ Adm
Hand-carved by Charle I.D. Looff Company in 1908.

3 Shelburne Museum
A vintage 1920s carousel that operates right outside the Shelburne Museum's Circus Building (*see p41*).

4 Crescent Park Carousel
MAP F4 ▪ 700 Bullocks Point Ave, East Providence, RI ▪ Adm
Charles I.D. Looff showcase.

5 Bushnell Park Carousel
MAP C4 ▪ Bushnell Park, Hartford, CT ▪ Adm
Beautiful three-row hand-carved wooden carousel.

6 Flying Horses Carousel
MAP G5 ▪ Oak Bluffs Ave, Oak Bluffs, Martha's Vineyard, MA ▪ Adm
1876–8 CWF Dare Company model.

7 Greenway Carousel
MAP X3 ▪ Boston, MA ▪ Adm
Carousel with hand-carved figures of local animals including a lobster.

8 Story Land
MAP M4 ▪ Rte 16, Glen, NH ▪ Adm
A strikingly unusual early 20th-century German carousel.

9 Heritage State Park
MAP C3 ▪ 221 Appleton St, Holyoke, MA ▪ Adm
This 1929 carousel has 20 standing horses and 28 jumpers.

10 Lighthouse Point Park
MAP C5 ▪ 2 Lighthouse Point Rd, New Haven, CT ▪ Adm
A 1916 carousel with 72 original figures.

🔟 New England Foods

1 Clams
It's easy to get confused by New England clams. "Quahog" is the Native-American name for the hard-shelled clam *Mercenaria mercenaria*, but the bivalve has other aliases. Small ones, known as "littlenecks," are served as the ever-popular battered-and-fried clam. Medium-sized quahogs are known as "cherrystones," and are often eaten raw. Big ones are stuffed and baked.

2 Maple Syrup
Nothing tames a Yankee sourpuss like pouring on the maple syrup over a stack of pancakes or waffles. In late winter, you might encounter sugar houses in the north of New England boiling down the sap of sugar maple trees. Stop for a jug – you'll never find it cheaper.

Maple syrup

3 Scallops
Scallops were popular in New England cooking long before they became a mainstay of gourmet restaurants. Look for them sautéed in butter, breaded and deep-fried, or tossed with linguine, herbs, and olive oil. Scallops are on almost every menu, not least because New Bedford, Massachusetts, lands more scallops than any other port in the world.

4 Cranberries
Popular in juices and muffins, cranberries are best known for the sugary sauce served as part of traditional Thanksgiving dinner. The state of Massachusetts still produces about a third of America's cranberry crop.

Fresh New England lobsters

5 Lobster
One of the pleasures of a New England summer is setting a steamed lobster on a picnic table, cracking it with a rock, and savoring the sweet meat with melted butter. *Homarus americanus*, often called "Maine lobster," is the world's largest crustacean, and is generally served at weights of 1¼–3 lb (0.5–1.3 kg).

6 Oysters
New England oysters are found on sandy bottoms all along the coast, but those cultured in beds near Damariscotta, Maine; Wellfleet, Massachusetts; and Norwalk, Connecticut, are celebrated for their delicate, distinctive flavors.

Oysters served on the half shell

7 Cheese
Visitors will find world-class farmstead cheeses all across New England. Small dairies make everything from fresh goat's milk chevre to aged, pungent blues. Somewhat larger Vermont cheese companies also produce superb American cheddar and Colby cheeses.

8 Blueberries
Whether you prefer the light blueberry accent of a muffin or the supreme intensity of a blueberry pie, there's no substitute for the tiny "wild" lowbush blueberry. Most wild blueberries are harvested in Maine from late July through August, but they freeze well, so blueberry baked treats are available all year.

Tray of blueberry muffins

9 Stone-ground Cornmeal
Order a jonnycake – a sweet cornmeal pancake cooked on a griddle – at any Rhode Island diner, and you'll be enjoying a culinary tradition going back to the region's first European colonists and the Native Americans before them.

10 Heirloom Apples
Look for orchard farmstands selling apples in the fall. Many historic apple varieties can be traced to their New England birthplace by name (Roxbury Russet, Westfield-Seek-No-Further). Preservation efforts begun in the 1980s have borne fruit in the widespread availability of dozens of historic varieties.

TOP 10 DRINKS

Green Mountain coffee

1 Green Mountain Coffee
The gourmet coffee roaster's blends are sold throughout the region.

2 Fresh Apple Cider
Freshly pressed and unfiltered apple juice is widely available in the fall.

3 Sam Adams Lager
The flagship brew of the Boston Beer Company launched the national craft beer revolution.

4 Del's Lemonade
A thirst-quenching Rhode Island favorite, this contains only lemon juice, sugar, and shaved ice.

5 Craft Brewed Cider
With the popularity of craft beers, small producers are now making many alcoholic craft ciders.

6 Coffee Milk
Rhode Island's official state drink is created by stirring coffee syrup into milk.

7 Sparkling Wines from Westport Rivers Winery
Estate-grown chardonnay and pinot noir grapes are used to make New England's best bubbly.

8 Moxie
Invented in 1876 by medical doctor Augustin Thompson, this soft drink with an appropriately medicinal aftertaste is now the official beverage of the state of Maine.

9 Lincoln Peak Vineyard Marquette
The signature red grape of this Vermont winery shows the triumph of artful winemaking over harsh climate.

10 Frappe
Pronounced "frap," this thick milkshake includes ice cream and syrup in true New England style.

⓾ Restaurants

1 Fore Street, Portland, ME

A handsome, exposed-brick dining room always filled with foodies. Wood-burning fires in the open kitchen cook and flavor fresh seafood and meats (see p129). Raw materials come from a community of Maine farmers, fishermen, foragers, and cheesemakers.

2 Menton, Boston, MA

This temple of French-Italian haute cuisine in the Boston Seaport is the flagship of chef-owner Barbara Lynch's culinary empire (see p83). Menton is noted for Lynch's imaginative seafood (including shrimp with chicory, almond, and horseradish), perfect service, and brilliant vintage wine pairings.

Foie gras with chestnuts, Menton

3 Ristorante Massimo, Portsmouth, NH

New England seafood acquires an Italian accent here, in this sophisticated dining room in a historic waterfront building (see p121). Don't miss the yellowfin tuna and lobster with lemon risotto.

4 Stars, Chatham, MA

Perhaps the most elegant special-occasion dining on Cape Cod, Stars emphasizes the bounty of the inn's own farm (see p85), the catch landed just feet away at Chatham Fish Pier, and superb dry-aged beef. The excellent wine list and cocktails are among the best on Cape Cod.

Exterior of Craigie On Main

5 Craigie On Main, MA

Chef Tony Maws, who is nationally acclaimed for his French-inspired nose-to-tail approach to fine dining, presides over a bustling open kitchen facing the dining area filled with an eclectic mix of diners. Head to the bar for its wildly popular gourmet burger (see p83).

6 Inn at Shelburne Farms Restaurant, VT

Inn guests always admire the Shelburne Farms market garden, and the food tastes as good as it looks (see p113). Produce that is sourced directly from this and other local farms is used to create a wonderful seasonal menu of classic Continental dishes with an American accent. Meals are served either in the elegant marble dining room or on the outdoor terrace.

The restaurant at Shelburne Farms

(7) Primo Restaurant, Rockland, ME

Freshness is key at this intimate coastal restaurant. The innovative menu depends on produce just pulled from the ground as well as local fish just pulled from the sea. The chef-owner raises her own produce *(see p129)* and makes the sausages from her own pigs.

(8) Al Forno, Providence, RI

A wood-fired oven provides the searing heat essential for cooking spectacular Northern Italian meat dishes like chorizo-stuffed quails with plum jam, as well as Al Forno's signature baked pasta dishes *(see p91)*. The style is Italian; most ingredients are local.

Tables at the Union League Café

(9) Union League Café, New Haven, CT

New England meat, produce, and spectacular fish get the French brasserie treatment at this classy but cozy dining spot at the edge of Yale University. There's also an outstanding raw bar of New England shellfish.

(10) Old Inn on the Green, New Marlborough, MA

Genuinely antique, the inn has no electricity, so candles light the tables and fireplaces glow in season *(see p85)*. There is nothing old-fashioned about the contemporary farm-to-table menus. Interestingly, all the produce is sourced from the chef's own farm.

TOP 10 PLACES TO EAT SEAFOOD

Abbott's Lobster in the Rough

1 Abbott's Lobster in the Rough
MAP D5 ▪ 860 536 7719 ▪ 117 Pearl St, Noank, CT
Butter-drenched lobster meat in a bun.

2 Woodman's of Essex
MAP G2 ▪ 978 768 6057 ▪ 121 Main St, Essex, MA
Their fried clams are among the best.

3 Evelyn's Drive-In
MAP F4 ▪ 401 624 3100 ▪ 2335 Main Rd, Tiverton, RI
Famous for their stuffed clams.

4 Barking Crab
MAP X4 ▪ 617 426 CRAB ▪ 88 Sleeper St, Boston, MA
Clam-shack ambience comes to the Boston waterfront.

5 Five Islands Lobster Co
MAP P4 ▪ 207 371 2990 ▪ 1447 Five Islands Rd, Georgetown, ME
Georgetown pier lobster shack.

6 Shaw's Fish & Lobster Wharf
Diners can watch lobster boats come and go in the narrow inlet *(see p128)*.

7 George's of Galilee
MAP E5 ▪ 401 783 2306 ▪ 250 Sand Hill Cove Rd, Galilee, RI
George's has had pick of the catch since 1948.

8 Net Result
MAP G5 ▪ 508 693 6071 ▪ 79 Beach Rd, Vineyard Haven, MA
Perfect fish. The menu varies with the catch of the day.

9 Lenny & Joe's Fish Tale
MAP D5 ▪ 860 669 0767 ▪ Rte 1, Westbrook, CT
Clear clam chowder with a hint of milk.

10 Bookstore Restaurant
MAP H4 ▪ 508 349 3154
▪ 50 Kendrick Ave, Wellfleet, MA
Oysters don't come any fresher.

Shopping Destinations

Brimfield antiques flea market

1 Brimfield, MA
MAP D3 ■ May, Jul, Sep ■ www.brimfieldantiquefleamarket.com
Whether you're seeking Art Deco jewelry or furniture crafted in Salem in the 1790s, Brimfield is the place to look. Antiques hunters from around the world converge on this small town for its three annual antiques shows in May, July, and September.

2 League of New Hampshire Craftsmen Fair, NH
MAP L5 ■ Mount Sunapee Resort, Newbury, NH ■ Early Aug ■ Adm ■ www.nhcrafts.org
Established in 1933, the League of New Hampshire Craftsmen Fair is the oldest craft fair in the US. More than 200 juried members and guest artists of the League offer their work, including jewelry, fine furniture, pottery, glass blowing, and weaving.

3 Woodbury, CT
MAP B5 ■ www.antiqueswoodbury.com
Dealers in fine American and British antiques set up shop here around half a century ago. They've since been joined by dealers in imported porcelain, Oriental rugs, and whatever is giving New York interior decorators shivers this season.

4 Shoppes at Buckland Hills, Manchester, CT
MAP C4 ■ 194 Buckland Hills Dr ■ www.theshoppesatbucklandhills.com
Central Connecticut's largest shopping area, this features virtually every big-box national chain store, including discount electronics, decor, and home goods dealers like the Christmas Tree Shop.

5 Providence Place, Providence, RI
MAP E4 ■ One Providence Pl ■ www.providenceplace.com
This mega-mall in downtown Providence has captured most of the retail activity in Rhode Island's capital. Stores occupy three levels, with entertainment and a food court above the shops.

6 Freeport, ME
MAP P4 ■ www.freeportusa.com
Outdoors outfitter L. L. Bean set the tone here when it opened in 1911. Freeport has since blossomed as a world-famous shopper's paradise; more than 100 shops offer the biggest and best name brands in American merchandising – often at substantial discounts.

The L. L. Bean store in Freeport

7 Manchester, VT
MAP K6 ■ www.manchester
designeroutlets.com

Two dozen high-fashion shops, such as Armani and Michael Kors, entice fans of upscale bargains to Manchester Designer Outlets. The town also has outdoor outfitters such as Orvis and Eddie Bauer.

8 Harvard Square, Cambridge, MA
MAP F2 ■ www.harvard
square.com

America's most literary city is home to two comprehensive bookstores, one of which prints out-of-print titles on demand. Also around Harvard Square are specialists in used books, poetry, and comic books.

Searching for books, Harvard Square

9 Weston, VT
General stores face each other across the main street in this picturesque village. The warren of rooms in the Vermont Country Store *(see p111)* contains all kinds of clever gadgets, outdoors apparel, cooking utensils, and an excellent selection of New England foods.

10 Wellfleet Flea Market & Drive-In, Wellfleet, MA
MAP H4 ■ Rte 6 ■ May–Sep ■ Adm
■ www.wellfleet cinemas.com/
flea-market

More than 200 vendors offer a mixture of trash and treasures, including the occasional antique, in the wide-open spaces of a drive-in theater near the end of Cape Cod.

TOP 10 SOUVENIRS

Red Sox baseball cap

1 Red Sox Baseball Cap
Show your loyalty in the epic rivalry between the Boston Red Sox and the New York Yankees.

2 Iconic Patriots Sweatshirt
Famed coach Bill Belichick is rarely seen in anything but the hooded gray New England Patriots sweatshirt.

3 Black Dog T-shirt
A black labrador T-shirt says "Martha's Vineyard" to anyone who has ever visited the Black Dog restaurant there.

4 Vermont Snow Globe
Capture winter permanently to set on your knickknack shelf.

5 Lobster Keychain
The bright crimson of New England's quintessential crustacean makes your keys easier to spot.

6 Pine-Scented Pillow
Mainers have been selling these fragrant headrests to tourists since steamships first started running in the 1830s.

7 "This Car Climbed Mount Washington" Bumper Sticker
People will regard your old clunker with new respect.

8 Nantucket Lightship Basket
True folk art commands high prices for basket-purses with fashion cachet.

9 Woody Jackson "Holy Cow" Art
Jackson's cow-themed art has cornered the market on the iconic black-and-white Vermont cows, with prints, cards, calendars, collectibles, and T-shirts.

10 Maine Tourmaline Jewelry
The most famous Western Maine tourmalines are "watermelon" stones with pink centers and green edges.

🔟 New England for Free

① Free Fun Fridays, MA
www.highlandstreet.org

Admission to ten different museums or cultural attractions throughout Massachusetts is free each Friday from late June until the end of August. See the website for institutions that take part.

② National Park Service Walking Tours, MA
MAP W3 ■ National Park Service Downtown Visitor Center, Faneuil Hall, 1 Faneuil Hall Sq, Boston ■ 617 242 5601 ■ Call for hours ■ www.nps.gov/bost

Park rangers offer a variety of free walking tours of Boston National Historical Park. They range from segments of the Freedom Trail to Charlestown Navy Yard.

③ Yale University Art Museums, New Haven, CT

The Yale University Art Gallery and the Yale Center for British Art have spectacular collections in landmark Louis B. Kahn buildings *(see p42)* from early and late in his career.

④ Green Mountain Trails, VT
MAP K3 ■ Green Mountain Club, 4711 Waterbury-Stowe Rd ■ 802 244 7037 ■ Open 9am–5pm daily (mid-Oct–mid-May: Mon–Fri) ■ www.greenmountainclub.org

Green Mountain Club's visitor center provides information, current trail conditions, and maps for hiking mountain trails all over Vermont.

⑤ Project Puffin Visitor Center, ME
MAP Q3 ■ 311 Main St, Rockland ■ 207 596 5566 ■ Open May: 10am–5pm Wed–Sun; Jun–Oct: 10am–5pm daily ■ www.projectpuffin.audubon.org

At the Project Puffin Visitor Center tourists can learn about the ongoing seabird restoration programs on Maine's offshore islands and experience live video and audio feeds of puffin rookeries – one of the great bird conservation success stories.

Town crier actor on Freedom Trail tour

⑥ Cliffwalk, RI
MAP F5 ■ Memorial Drive to Ochre Point, Newport ■ 401 849 8048 ■ www.cliffwalk.com

This 3.5-mile (5.5-km) walk above the natural rocky shore skirts the backyards of some of Newport's most dramatic Gilded Age mansions. Parts of the southern half are on a rough trail.

⑦ Hampton Beach Concerts and Fireworks, NH
MAP N6 ■ 115 Ocean Blvd, Hampton Beach ■ www.hamptonbeach.org ■ Jun–Aug

Every night throughout the summer free concerts of various music

Indo-Pacific galleries, Yale Art Gallery

genres are held on Hampton Beach, capped off each Wednesday with a display of fireworks at 9:30pm.

8 Boston Public Library Tours, MA
MAP U4 ▪ Copley Sq, Boston ▪ 617 536 5400 ▪ Call for opening hours ▪ www.bpl.org

Docents lead informative tours of the splendid art and architecture in Boston Public Library, which is also known as the "palace of the people."

Hickory trees, Arnold Arboretum

9 Arnold Arboretum, MA
MAP F3 ▪ 125 Arborway, Boston

Established in 1872, this combined botanical research facility and public park features 281 acres (114 ha) of rolling landscape crisscrossed with walking trails. The scent of lilac fills the air in May, but it's the vibrant foliage of broadleaf trees in September and October that really draws the crowds here.

10 WaterFire, Providence, RI

Braziers floating on canals create a magical aura around the Providence waterfront for concerts and citywide celebration (see p72). Check the website for the schedule of events.

TOP 10 MONEY-SAVING TIPS

Red Sox team member

1 The Red Sox farm-team games in Worcester, MA cost much less than a game at Fenway (www.milb.com/worcester).

2 In Boston, BosTix booths at Copley Square and Faneuil Hall sell discounted theater, music, dance, and comedy tickets (www.artsboston.org.bostix).

3 MBTA weekly passes offer big savings on subway and bus fares in and around Boston (www.mbta.com).

4 Many museums and hotels offer discounts to seniors, students, or members of AAA.

5 Many museums offer a period of free admission each week. Check their websites for details.

6 Purchase fuel from Tuesday to Thursday for the week's lowest prices.

7 The America the Beautiful Pass covers admission and fees at more than 2,000 federal recreation sites (www.nps.gov/findapark/passes.htm).

8 Inquire about special family rates at attractions and museums.

9 Lunch is more affordable than dinner at New England's top restaurants.

10 Purchase cheap lunches or picnic ingredients at farmers' markets.

Farmers' market apples

🔟 Festivals and Events

1 Winter Carnival, Stowe, VT
MAP K3 ■ Stowe, VT ■ 802 253 7321 ■ late Jan ■ www.stowewinter carnival.com

Plummeting temperatures and falling snow are celebrated with snow golf, snow volleyball, and ice-carving.

2 Patriot's Day
MAP E2 ■ Lexington and Concord, MA ■ 978 369 6993 ■ 3rd Mon in Apr ■ www.nps.gov/mima

This re-enactment of the opening salvos of the American Revolution starts before dawn in Lexington and continues on to nearby Concord.

3 WaterFire, Providence, RI
MAP E4 ■ Providence, RI ■ 401 273 1155 ■ May–Nov ■ Donation ■ www.waterfire.org

Nothing epitomizes the renaissance of the Providence waterfront as well as WaterFire, an environmental sculpture by Barnaby Evans. Its 80 floating bonfires, on the city's three downtown rivers, make a magical setting for a host of summer arts events.

4 Jazz and Folk Festivals, Newport, RI
MAP F5 ■ Newport, RI ■ Summer ■ Adm ■ newportjazz.org; www.newportfolk.org

For over 50 years, these festivals have been a focus for fresh talent as well as for star performers. Fort Adams State Park, set at the mouth of the harbor with panoramic views of Newport Bridge and the East Passage, makes a perfect venue.

5 International Festival of Arts & Ideas, New Haven, CT
MAP C5 ■ New Haven, CT ■ 888 278 4332 ■ mid-Jun ■ www.artidea.org

Every June, New Haven holds hundreds of events, the majority free, including opera on New Haven Green, hip-hop poets, dance, and readings by Nobel Laureate authors.

6 Windjammer Days, Boothbay Harbor, ME
MAP P4 ■ Boothbay Harbor, ME ■ 207 633 2353 ■ late Jun ■ www.windjammerdays.org

Seven days of family fun include windjammer cruise schooners and other tall ships in Boothbay Harbor, an antique boat parade, waterfront concerts, a craft fair, and fireworks.

7 Green River Festival, Greenfield, MA
MAP C2 ■ Check website for location ■ late Jun ■ Adm ■ www.green riverfestival.com

The Green River festival is a combination of hot-air ballooning and music, featuring folk, bluegrass, Americana, indie rock, Cajun,

Chick Corea, Newport Jazz Festival

Hot-air balloons, Green River Festival

and zydeco music in a fairground venue. On-site camping pitches are available.

8 Independence Day Celebrations

Bristol, RI: MAP F4; www.fourth ofjulybristolri.com ■ Boston, MA: MAP F2; www.bostonpopsjuly4th.org

The red-white-and-blue stripe marks the Fourth of July parade route in Bristol, site of one of the most enthusiastic small-town parades in the US. The televised Independence Day celebration in Boston is famous for its fireworks and Boston Pops concert.

9 Maine Lobster Festival

MAP Q3 ■ Rockland, ME ■ 800 576 7512 ■ late Jul–early Aug ■ Adm ■ www.mainelobsterfestival.com

More than 20,000 lb (9,000 kg) of lobster are steamed every year for this Rockland waterfront festival. Lobstermen race across floating crates, floats parade down the street, and a beauty pageant chooses a Sea Goddess to preside over the event.

10 Thanksgiving Celebration, Plymouth, MA

MAP G3 ■ Plymouth, MA ■ 508 747 7525 ■ 4th Thu in Nov ■ www.see plymouth.com

Locals, some heirs to *Mayflower* pilgrims re-enact the Thanksgiving of 1621. Another ceremony highlights original Native American culture.

TOP 10 AGRICULTURAL FAIRS

1 Woodstock Fair
MAP D4 ■ South Woodstock, CT ■ late Aug–early Sep
Long-established harvest celebration and rural home-coming.

2 Cheshire Fair
MAP L6 ■ 247 Monadnock Hwy, Swanzey, NH ■ late Jul–early Aug
Pony pulls, puppets, pie-eating, and country music.

3 Addison County Fair & Field Days
MAP J4 ■ 1790 Field Days Rd, New Haven, VT ■ early Aug
Vermont's largest agricultural fair.

4 Washington County Fair
MAP E5 ■ Rte 112, Richmond, RI ■ mid–late Aug
Don't miss the rooster-crowing contest.

5 Brooklyn Fair
MAP D4 ■ Rte 169, Brooklyn, CT ■ late Aug
Nashville entertainment, old-fashioned midway rides, and prize poultry.

6 Barnstable County Fair
MAP G5 ■ Rte 151, E Falmouth, MA ■ mid-Jul
Demolition derby and bull-riding top the entertainment here.

7 Champlain Valley Fair
MAP J3 ■ Essex Junction, VT ■ late Aug–early Sep
From extreme motorcycle show to sheep and dairy exhibits.

8 Eastern States Exposition
MAP C3 ■ 1305 Memorial Ave, West Springfield, MA ■ mid-Sep–Oct
New England's largest fair.

9 Fryeburg Fair
MAP M4 ■ Fryeburg, ME ■ early Oct
This traditional agricultural fair also features woodsmen competitions.

10 Topsfield Fair
MAP F2 ■ Topsfield, MA ■ early Oct
Farmers have gathered here since 1818.

Fairgoers at Woodstock

New England Area by Area

Lighthouse at Portland Head, Maine

TOP 10 **Massachusetts**

Massachusetts is where English settlers first imagined remaking their homeland in a wilderness they called New England. For all their Englishness, they named the bay between Cape Cod and the mainland after the coastal Massachusett people, then took the bay's name for their colony. The towns of Plymouth, Salem, and Boston were the beachhead from which the rest of New England was colonized. As the state with the first college, first democratic government, first rebels to defy the king, first authors to invent an American literature, and the first sailors to open the ports of Asia to the West, Massachusetts claims that much of what matters about New England happened here first. The state remains a pioneer of science and culture to this day.

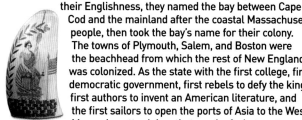

Whaling Museum, Nantucket

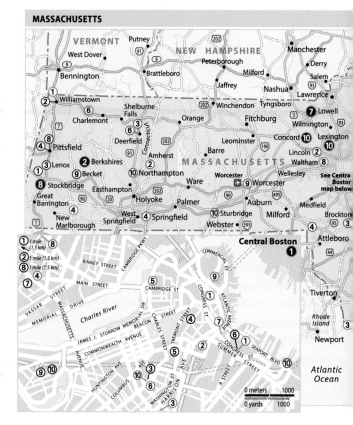

Historic Acorn Street, Boston

Historic Boston
① New England's largest city, Boston is nicknamed "the Hub," not just because all New England roads do eventually lead here, but because Bostonians think of their home as the center of all things historical,

intellectual, and cultural in the region (see pp12–13). Rightly so; Boston's history is inevitably the lead tale in New England's development.

Berkshires
② Almost equidistant from Boston to the east and New York City to the south, the Berkshire Hills pledge a wavering allegiance to both. But the Berkshires is a valley kingdom unto itself. Its summer social schedule revolves around the performing arts (see pp32–3), but the concentration of resident artists guarantees a rich off-season as well.

Martha's Vineyard
③ MAP G5

The fish-shaped island of Martha's Vineyard covers 100 sq miles (259 sq km) yet is only 7 miles (11 km) off the mainland. Up Island, the rustic western end, is a serene natural world that includes the sacred striped clay banks of Aquinnah. Down Island, the bustling eastern end, has the town of Vineyard Haven, the old whaling port of Edgartown, and the camp-meeting resort of Oak Bluffs.

Cliffs of Aquinnah, Martha's Vineyard

New Bedford
④ MAP F4

Settled in 1640, this deepwater port at the mouth of Buzzards Bay has always wrested its living from the sea. In the 1840s, pine-masted whaling barks would tie up at the wharves to offload whale oil from a three-year journey (see p46). Today that harbor creaks with great iron fishing boats that dredge Georges Bank for scallops, haul flounder from Nantucket Shoals, or venture offshore for cod.

5 Plymouth

MAP G3 ▪ Pilgrim Hall
Museum: 75 Court St, Plymouth;
508 746 1620; open Feb–Dec:
10am–5pm Wed–Sat; adm;
www.pilgrimhall.org

Plymouth calls itself "America's
home town," as it was the first
English settlement in New England
and home of the Separatists, who
became known as Pilgrims. The
living history museum of Plimoth
Pautuxet (see p38) depicts the
settlement around 1627, and
also has exhibits devoted
to Wampanoag life in the
same era. History is
marked with a statue or
plaque on almost every
corner. Pilgrim Hall
Museum displays Pilgrim-
era artifacts. Exhibitions
explore Native American
history and culture.

6 Cape Cod

English explorer
Bartholomew Gosnold
literally put Cape Cod on
the map in 1602 when he
named the long curl of land for the
fish so abundant in its waters. Cape
Cod's soils are but 15,000 years old –
composed of the sand and gravel
that mark the southernmost advance
of the last glacier – and it is hardly
terra firma; every large storm subtly
reshapes the shore, making peninsulas into islands and vice versa. Yet
the very transience of Cape Cod is
part of its allure (see pp16–17).

Cape Cod, jutting out into the Atlantic

WITCH TRIALS

Salem exhibits mixed feelings about its
witch history. On the 300th anniversary
of the 1692 hysteria that led to the
hanging of 19 "witches" and crushing
of another, the city erected a solemn
memorial to the victims. But come
Halloween, Salem is "witch city,"
capitalizing on its sensational past
to draw curious visitors.

**Artifact at Pilgrim
Hall Museum,
Plymouth**

7 Lowell

MAP F2

Lowell was the first
purpose-built city
in the US, con-
structed in the 1820s
as a large factory town
to manufacture textiles with
equipment designs adapted
from British mills. The textile
industry is gone, but the canal
network and looming mills
remain as testament to the
country's first tryst with the
Industrial Revolution (see
p39). After you've soaked
up the mill history, visit
Jack Kerouac Park (part
of Lowell National Historical Park)
to pay your respects to the Beat
author who was a native son.

8 Nantucket

MAP H5

In contrast with Martha's Vineyard,
only residents bother to bring a car
to tiny Nantucket, as the island lies
30 miles (48 km) offshore and
transportation is expensive. Even
residents tend to bicycle everywhere
(tourists on scooters are scorned).

Explore venerable gray-shingled Nantucket town on foot, starting at the whaling museum (see p46). Then bike to Wauwinet to hike the dunes at Great Point, to Siasconset to see rose-covered cottages, or Surfside to swim or fly kites on the beach.

9 **Salem**
MAP F2

In the popular imagination, Salem is the city that tried and executed witches. But the 1692 trials are best seen as an aberration in the history of this vibrant city blessed with the art of the Peabody Essex Museum (see p41) and a rich maritime history recounted in the Salem Maritime National Historic Site (see p47). In the early days of the country, Salem's merchant princes were richer than the national treasury. Their grand houses still attest to their power.

Salem Witch Museum

10 **Concord and Lexington**
MAP E2, F2 ■ Ralph Waldo Emerson House: 28 Cambridge Tpk, Concord; 978 369 2236; open mid-Apr–Oct: 10am–4:30pm Thu–Sat, 1–4pm Sun; adm

The opening skirmishes of the American Revolution, in what is now Minute Man National Historical Park (see p38), forever link these neighboring towns. Concord also gave the US its first literary voices in Ralph Waldo Emerson (1803–82) and Henry David Thoreau (1817–62). Also, novelist Louisa May Alcott (1832–88) grew up in Orchard House (see p44). All of the above are buried at Concord's Sleepy Hollow Cemetery.

A DAY PEDALING FROM CAMBRIDGE TO CONCORD

▶ MORNING

Start your 13-mile (21-km) jaunt through American history by taking your bike with you on the T to the Alewife terminus of the Red Line. Follow well-marked signs to the **Minuteman Bikeway**, a flat, paved path. Pedal through Arlington, then watch for egrets, and herons along the edges of **Great Meadows** nature area. The bikeway passes the **Lexington Visitors' Center** of Minute Man National Historical Park (see p38), perfect for a rest stop. Pick up the park map and brochures, taking note of historic **Lexington Green**, your next stop. See Daniel Chester French's famed Minute Man statue on the green, then pedal a few blocks up Bedford Street to grab a box lunch at **Neillio's Gourmet Kitchen** (No. 53).

AFTERNOON

Just west of Lexington Green you switch from the Minuteman Bikeway to **Battle Road Trail**, an unpaved road for walkers and cyclists that parallels the route of the running battle as British forces retreated in 1775; historical signposts explain the significance of sights along the way. **North Bridge**, near another visitor center in the park, is especially evocative. At the end of the trail, follow signs to **The Wayside** and **Orchard House** (see p44) to learn about Concord's 19th-century literary history. Lexington Road takes you into Concord Center, where you and your bike can return to Boston on the commuter rail.

See map on pp76–7

The Best of the Rest

1 Gloucester
MAP G2

Sticking 30 miles (42 km) out to sea on Cape Ann, Gloucester's harbor is a legendary fishing port and home to Rocky Neck Art Colony (see p84).

2 Northampton and Amherst
MAP C3

The vibrant cultural life of Pioneer Valley revolves around four colleges, including Smith, with its major art museum (see p42). Literary history abounds, as the Emily Dickinson Homestead in Amherst attests.

3 Deerfield and the Connecticut Valley
MAP C2 ■ Historic Deerfield: Old Main Street, Old Deerfield; 413 774 5581; open mid-Apr–late Dec: 9:30am–4:30pm daily; Jan–mid-Apr: call for hours; adm; www.historic-deerfield.org

Raids during the Seven Years War did not deter settlers from the rich valley soil here. Deerfield has 60 buildings from the 17th and 18th centuries.

4 Springfield
MAP C3 ■ 800 625 7738
■ www.springfieldmuseums.org

The Dr. Seuss Museum at the Quadrangle off State Street complements outdoor Seuss sculptures and adjacent art, history, and natural science museums.

5 Rockport
MAP G2

The iconic Motif #1, a red fishing shed in the harbor, is among the most-painted subjects in this lovely village of art galleries and boutiques.

6 Mohawk Trail
MAP C2 ■ www.mohawktrail.com

Drive Route 2 west from Greenfield over the Berkshire Mountains to North Adams to be wowed by foliage. Turnoffs lead to orchards, river rafting, mountain hiking, and sugar houses.

7 Ipswich and Essex
MAP F2, G2

The sands of Crane Beach (see p52) in Ipswich and the winding tidal river at Essex (see p84) make these North Shore communities great for nature lovers. Both are famed for shellfish.

8 Newburyport
MAP N6

Its fantastic concentration of grand Federal-style homes makes Newburyport an essential stop for history buffs and preservationists. Birders flock to Plum Island at the harbor mouth for some of New England's best birding.

9 Worcester
MAP E3 ■ EcoTarium: 222 Harrington Way, Worcester; 508 929 2700; open 10am–5pm Tue–Sat, noon–5pm Sun; adm; www.ecotarium.org

Worcester has a top art museum (see p40) and a unique indoor-outdoor museum, the EcoTarium.

10 Brimfield and Sturbridge
MAP D3

New England's rural heart bustles thrice a year with Brimfield antiques shows (see p68). Old Sturbridge Village (see p38) re-creates rural New England of 150 years ago.

Motif #1 in Rockport's harbor

Summer Performing Arts

1 Tanglewood
MAP B3 ■ 297 West St, Lenox
■ 888 266 1200 ■ late Jun–early Sep
■ Adm ■ www.bso.org
Supreme musicianship and
elaborate picnics are equally
characteristic of the Boston
Symphony's summer home.

Williamstown Theatre Festival

2 Williamstown Theatre Festival
MAP B2 ■ 1000 Main St, Williamstown
■ 413 458 3200 ■ Jun–Aug ■ Adm
■ www.wtfestival.org
Film and TV directors and actors
come here to hone their stagecraft;
celebrity-spotting is a summer sport
in town when the festival takes place.

3 Shakespeare & Company
MAP B3 ■ 70 Kemble St, Lenox ■ 413
637 3353 ■ late May–mid Sep ■ Adm
■ www.shakespeare.org
Famed for their Shakespeare
performances, this company also
develops and produces new plays
of social and political significance.

4 Barrington Stage Company
MAP B2 ■ 30 Union St, Pittsfield ■ 413
236 8888 ■ mid-Jun–Oct ■ Adm
■ www.barringtonstageco.org
A wellspring of new plays and
musicals, Barrington Stage incu-
bates electrifying theater that often
winds up playing on Broadway.

5 Gloucester Stage Company
MAP G2 ■ 267 E Main St, Gloucester
■ 978 281 4433 ■ May–Oct ■ Adm
■ www.gloucesterstage.com
Founded in 1979, this award-winning
theatre company, next to Rocky Neck
Art Colony stages socially relevant
dramas, comedies and musicals.

6 Wellfleet Harbor Actors Theater
MAP H4 ■ Rte 6, Wellfleet
■ 508 349 9428 ■ May–Oct ■ Adm
■ www.what.org
Humor, passion, a sense of the
absurd, and a sharp political edge
are hallmarks of this small troupe.

7 Cape Playhouse
MAP H4 ■ 820 Rte 6A,
Dennis ■ 508 385 3911 ■ mid-Jun–
Oct, 2nd half Dec ■ Adm ■ www.
capeplayhouse.com
America's oldest professional
summer theater puts on classics,
comedies, mysteries, and musicals.

8 Berkshire Theatre Group
MAP B3 ■ Main St, Stockbridge ■ 413
997 4444 ■ mid-Jun–Oct ■ Adm
■ www.berkshiretheatregroup.org
The 1888 Stockbridge Casino and
Pittsfield's 1910 Colonial Theatre
make grand settings for new, classic,
and contemporary theater.

9 Jacob's Pillow Dance Festival
MAP B3 ■ 358 George Carter Rd,
Becket ■ 413 243 9919 ■ mid-Jun–late
Aug ■ Adm ■ www.jacobspillow.org
Enjoy performances by leading US
and international dance companies
in a magical setting.

10 Leader Bank Pavilion
MAP F2 ■ 290 Northern Ave,
Boston ■ 617 728 1600 ■ Jun–early
Sep ■ Adm ■ www.livenation.com
This harborside pavilion is a dynamic
venue for various performers.

See map on pp76–7

Places to Shop

 Faneuil Hall Marketplace

MAP X3 ▪ Boston

North and South Markets boast dozens of boutiques and specialty shops. Quincy Market has the city's best food court, as well as more than 40 pushcart vendors selling largely local wares.

 deCordova Museum Store

MAP F2 ▪ 51 Sandy Pond Rd, Lincoln

Contemporary art, mostly by New England artists, is the focus of deCordova Sculpture Park and Museum. The store at the museum matches that spirit with a range of art supplies, jewelry, wearable art, and toys.

 Fuller Craft Museum

MAP F3 ▪ 455 Oak St, Brockton

This premier museum of fine art in craft media carries an extensive selection of artists' jewelry, which is displayed alongside work in glass, ceramic, fiber, and wood.

 Wrentham Village Premium Outlets

MAP F3 ▪ 1 Premium Outlets Blvd, Wrentham

Bargain hunters from all over New England converge on this mall just off I-495, where 170 stores are dedicated to designer apparel and upscale housewares.

 Rocky Neck Art Colony

MAP G2

It is not difficult to see why this rocky peninsula is such an inspiration to artists. You can walk from cottage to cottage to see (and buy) paintings created by resident painters who belong to one of the oldest operating art colonies in America.

 Yankee Candle Village

MAP C2 ▪ Rtes 5 & 10, South Deerfield

The leading US producer of scented candles offers the world's largest candle selection, home furnishings, food, entertainment, all-year Christmas shopping, and custom candle-making.

 Sandwich Glass Museum

MAP G4 ▪ 129 Main St, Sandwich

Sandwich Glass Museum

The museum shop carries faithful reproductions of historic pressed glass from Sandwich, an extensive line of American art glass, and blown glass from the museum's own on-site glassblowing studio.

 Essex

MAP G2

More than a dozen antiques shops do business in this historic North Shore community. Keep an eye out to find nautical artifacts, Chinese export porcelain, 18th- and 19th-century furniture, and excellent oil paintings.

Provincetown

MAP H3

In summer, Friday is "gallery night" in Provincetown. Galleries along Commercial Street set out wine and cheese to lure prospective buyers.

Paradise City Arts Festivals

MAP C3 ▪ Rte 9 and Old Ferry Rd, Northampton

Two of the largest gatherings of crafts artists and designers in New England take place over Memorial Day (late May) and Columbus Day (mid-October) weekends at the Three-County Fairgrounds in Northampton, an excellent opportunity to explore and buy local crafts.

Restaurants

PRICE CATEGORIES

For a three course meal for one with half a bottle of wine (or equivalent meal), taxes and extra charges.

$ under $40 $$ $40–$65 $$$ over $65

1 Mezze Bistro + Bar
MAP B2 ■ 777 Cold Spring Rd, Williamstown ■ 413 458 0123 ■ Closed L ■ $$

Local growers provide the meat, produce, and cheeses for this highly adept American bistro.

2 Cape Sea Grille
MAP H4 ■ 31 Sea St, Harwich Port ■ 508 432 4745 ■ Closed Jan–mid-Apr, L & some days spring and fall ■ $$

Great local fish meets Cape Cod veggies to spectacular effect for elegant, candlelit dining.

3 Back Eddy
MAP F4 ■ 1 Bridge Rd, Westport ■ 508 636 6500 ■ Closed Mon–Fri L, Jan–Mar ■ $$

Casual cuisine and a raw bar serving Westport shellfish and wood-grilled local meats and fish. The outdoor bar is a convival social scene.

Delicious steamed clams

4 Old Inn on the Green, New Marlborough, MA
MAP B3 ■ 134 Hartsville–New Marlboro Rd ■ 413 229 7924 ■ Closed L, Mon & Tue Nov–Jun ■ $$$

Dine by candlelight in the four dining rooms of this 18th-century inn. The contemporary American bistro offers fresh and exciting fare.

5 Topper's
MAP H5 ■ 120 Wauwinet Rd, Nantucket ■ 508 228 0145 ■ Closed late Oct–Apr ■ $$$

In an idyllic waterfront setting, gorge on the succulent Beef Wellington, skillet-roasted halibut, or buttered lobster in a truffle emulsion.

6 Sweet Life Café
MAP G5 ■ 63 Circuit Ave, Oak Bluffs, Martha's Vineyard ■ 508 696 0200 ■ Closed L, Mon–Wed May & Sep–Oct, Nov–Apr ■ $$$

Local vegetables and fish feature on the seasonal menu with French, Italian, and Spanish accents matched by an extensive wine list.

7 Duckworth's Bistrot
MAP G2 ■ 197 E Main St, Gloucester ■ 978 282 4426 ■ Closed L, Mon, Sun Sep–May, Jan ■ $$

The French-trained chef-owner offers sumptuous bistro fare – grilled strip steak, duck breast with apples, and seafood stew.

8 Il Capriccio
MAP F2 ■ 888 Main St, Waltham ■ 781 894 2234 ■ Closed L, Sun ■ $$

The elegant Northern Italian menu changes often, depending on the New England harvest and the fishermen's catch. Extensive wine list.

9 Ledger
MAP F2 ■ 125 Washington St, Salem ■ 978 594 1908 ■ Open for brunch Sat & Sun, D Wed–Sun ■ $$$

Housed in an old bank, this upscale casual bistro serves New England cuisine made with the finest local ingredients.

10 Stars, Chatham, MA
MAP H4 ■ Chatham Bars Inn, 297 Shore Rd ■ 508 945 0096 ■ Hours vary with season ■ $$$

This four-star Cape Cod restaurant serves traditional steakhouse fare and excellent seafood. Don't forget to try the creative dessert menu.

See map on pp76–7

Bars and Nightlife in Boston

1 The Sinclair
MAP F2 ▪ 52 Church St, Cambridge
Part gastropub and part music venue, The Sinclair serves bistro comfort fare as indie bands, Americana musicians, and hipster songwriters entertain.

2 Regattabar
MAP F2 ▪ Charles Hotel, 1 Bennett St, Cambridge
This intimate room that boasts excellent acoustics is widely acclaimed for presenting some of the best jazz in the country.

3 Beehive
MAP V5 ▪ 541 Tremont St
This Bohemian bar-café programs live jazz by local artists. The creative bistro menu is complemented by craft beers and exotic cocktails.

The glamorous Yvonne's

4 Yvonne's
MAP W4 ▪ 2 Winter Place
One of Boston's most legendary dining spots exudes old-school elegance. The opulent interior, including a restored 19th-century vintage bar, add glamour to the innovative and classic cocktails.

5 Nick's Comedy Stop
MAP V4 ▪ 100 Warrenton St
Nationally known comics from HBO, Showtime, Comedy Central, MTV, and the like headline at this popular spot, which is Boston's longest-running comedy club (since 1977).

Drink, a cocktail landmark

6 Drink
MAP X4 ▪ 348 Congress St
Fresh herbs, hand-chipped ice, and specialty liqueurs place this hip bar in the vanguard of the cocktail world. Bartenders ask you your mood and then improvise a drink.

7 Middle East
MAP S3 ▪ 472–480 Massachusetts Ave, Cambridge
If you follow underground music, you're probably already aware of this legendary venue for new bands that are looking to break through.

8 The Plough & the Stars
MAP W3 ▪ 912 Massachusetts Ave, Cambridge
Founded in 1969, this musical bar is where Van Morrison penned part of his *Astral Weeks* album. There is live music from Thursday to Saturday.

9 Game On
MAP S5 ▪ 82 Lansdowne St
One of sports-crazy Boston's top game-watching spots is built into the walls of Fenway Park. With an entire wall covered with flat-screen TVs, there's always, well, a game on.

10 House of Blues®
MAP S5 ▪ 15 Lansdowne St
The famed chain sticks to its Boston roots with this cavernous venue.

See map on pp76–7

Restaurants in Boston

PRICE CATEGORIES

For a three course meal for one with half
a bottle of wine (or equivalent meal),
taxes and extra charges.

....

$ under $40   **$$** $40–$65   **$$$** over $65

1 Menton
MAP X4 ■ 354 Congress St
■ 617 737 0099 ■ Closed L daily ■ $$$
South Boston-raised Barbara Lynch
artfully reinvents fine dining at the
cusp of French and Italian.

2 Oya
MAP W4 ■ 9 East St ■ 617 654
9900 ■ Closed L daily & Sun–Mon ■ $$$
This modernJapanese restaurant is
celebrated for chef Tim Cushman's
inventive sushi and *omakase*.

3 Gaslight
MAP V6 ■ 600 Harrison Ave
■ 617 451 0560 ■ Closed L ■ $$
French bistro fare runs the gamut
from great steak-frites to roasted
lamb shanks, or a New England take
on bouillabaisse. The menu also has
a good selection of signature cocktails.

4 Craigie On Main
MAP S3 ■ 853 Main St ■ 617
497 5511 ■ $$$
Home of the wildly popular gourmet
burger. Local chef Tony Maws follows
a no-exceptions policy on local, seasonal, and organic ingredients.

5 Scampo, Liberty Hotel
MAP V3 ■ 215 Charles St
■ 617 536 2100 ■ $$$
The chefs here conjure fine
contemporary American food
with a New England accent.

6 B+G Oysters
MAP V5 ■ 550 Tremont St
■ 617 423 0550 ■ $$
At least a dozen varieties of oyster
are available here, and the sparkling
and mineral-rich white wines recommended are a perfect match.

7 Trade
MAP X4 ■ 540 Atlantic Ave ■ 617
451 1234 ■ Closed L Sat, Sun ■ $$
Trade is the fine-dining anchor to
Greenway Park that links Downtown
and the waterfront. It is a hotspot for
Mediterranean-inspired bites, craft
beers, and designer cocktails.

8 Oleana
MAP S2 ■ 134 Hampshire St,
Cambridge ■ 617 661 0505 ■ Closed L
■ $$$
Expect Arab-inspired eastern
Mediterranean cuisines at Oleana,
featuring spicy dishes from Turkey,
Greece, and North Africa. Many
diners choose to sit at the outdoor
tables in the garden.

9 Mare Oyster Bar
MAP X3 ■ 3 Mechanic St
■ 617 723 6273 ■ Closed L ■ $$
Local oysters and crudo plates
complement Italian seafood dishes
in this chic North End restaurant.

10 Banyan Bar + Refuge
MAP V5 ■ 553 Tremont St
■ 617 556 5611 ■ Closed L, open Sun
brunch ■ $$
This modern Asian gastropub hits
all the marks with Phillip Tang's
skillful blend of East and West.

Asian-inspired Banyan Bar

🔟 Rhode Island

Rhode Island is not an island at all, but it claims more than its share of dramatic rocky cliffs, sandy beaches, and languid riverbanks. The state was founded by religious dissenters from Massachusetts who chafed at the orthodoxies of Boston and Salem Puritans. The smallest US state, Rhode Island is divided by the very large, fan-shaped Narragansett Bay. At the head of the bay, the capital city of Providence revels in both its Colonial history and its futuristic outlook – the latter courtesy of its colleges and universities. The South County coastline west of the bay features idyllic barrier beaches with long, golden strands and fertile marshes trapped behind high dunes. The mouth of the bay is crossed by stepping-stone islands (and magnificent bridges) that lead to the first home of the US Navy, now the yachting capital of Newport.

Lighthouse, Point Judith

RHODE ISLAND

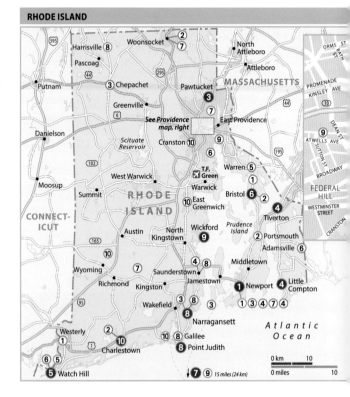

Modern buildings dominating the skyline of Providence

1 Newport

Nineteenth-century mansions and a snug harbor dotted with racing yachts and speedboats make this city one of the great American summer destinations. The downtown area is a history buff's delight *(see pp18–19)*.

2 Providence
MAP E4

Rhode Island School of Design (RISD) *(see pp42, 93)*, a top US art school, provides zing to downtown Providence, a city also known as a major dining destination. Benefit Street's "Mile of History" captures in its museums and historic houses 250 years of New England life. Visit the traditionally Italian district of Federal Hill for restaurants, salumerias, and coffee shops.

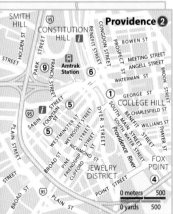

The historic Slater Mill at Pawtucket

3 Pawtucket
MAP E4

So close to Providence that it's hard to distinguish the two, Pawtucket flourished because it sits at the mouth of the Blackstone River, the storied stream of 19th-century industry that drains central New England. Samuel Slater opened the country's first successful cotton mill *(see p39)* here in 1793, jump-starting the American Industrial Revolution. Today it is best known for the vast Rhode Island Antiques Mall, and its September Dragon Boat Race.

Sakonnet Vineyard, Little Compton

4 Tiverton/Little Compton
MAP F4, F5 ■ Carolyn's
Sakonnet Vineyard: 162 W Main Rd,
Little Compton; 401 635 8486; open
late May–mid-Oct: 11am–6pm daily
(to 8pm Fri–Sat); mid-Oct–late May:
11am–5pm daily; www.sakonnet
wine.com

Occupying their own little peninsula
between Narragansett Bay and the
Massachusetts border, Tiverton (see
p48) and Little Compton are insulated
from the modern world by woods and
rolling farmland. Watch for roadside
stands selling seasonal strawberries
and sweet corn. Wine grapes also
flourish. Visit Carolyn's Sakonnet
Vineyard for tours and tastings.

5 Watch Hill
MAP E5

The glorious beaches of South
County, the Rhode Island shore west
of Point Judith, reach their apogee at
Watch Hill, an old-fashioned seaside
community of the town of Westerly.
The village also boasts the charming
Flying Horse Carousel.

6 Bristol
MAP F4 ■ Herreshoff Marine
Museum: 1 Burnside St; 401 253
5000; open Apr–mid-Dec: 10am–5pm
daily; adm; www.herreshoff.org
■ Blithewold Mansion & Gardens: 101
Ferry Rd; 401 253 2707; open May–
Oct: 10am–4pm Tue–Sat, until 3pm
Sun; late Nov–Dec: 11am–5pm Tue–
Sun; gardens year round; adm; www.
blithewold.org

Renowned for jubilant Independence
Day celebrations that date from

1785 (see p72), Bristol is a charming
deep-water seaport on the east side
of Narragansett Bay. The village is
home to the Herreshoff yacht-building
firm, whose museum traces the
history of the America's Cup, the
most prestigious prize in yacht-
racing. Visit the Blithewold estate,
where Rhode Island brides flock
to wed with spectacular vistas of
Narragansett Bay as a backdrop.

7 Block Island
MAP E6 ■ Block Island
Ferry: Pt Judith; 401 783 7996;
www.blockislandferry.com

Just 15 miles (24 km) off the coast,
Block Island has long been a summer
vacation haven for New Englanders. A
quarter of its land is protected against
development (zoning prohibits modern
structures), and 30 miles (48 km) of
nature trails crisscross the pear-
shaped island. Crescent Beach, just
north of the Victorian resort village of
Old Harbor, has fabulous swimming
and – when the wind is right – good
surfing. Deep-sea fishing excursions
are popular day-trips from Old Harbor.

8 Narragansett/Point Judith
MAP E5

In 1900, a fire destroyed the hotels
and casino that made Narragansett
Beach a high-society resort. Today,
families and sunbathers rule the

CLAIBORNE PELL BRIDGE

Constructed 1966–9, Newport's
Claiborne Pell Bridge is the longest
bridge in Rhode Island and the largest
suspension bridge in New England. With
a main span of 1,601 ft (488 m) and an
overall length of 11,247 ft (3,428 m), the
bridge arcs over Narragansett Bay to
connect Jamestown and Newport.

beach while surfers in wetsuits ride the waves. The peninsula going south ends at Point Judith, which shelters the fishing port of Galilee. Whale-watching and deep-sea-fishing cruise vessels share berths with the fishing boats. Don't miss fish dinner at George's of Galilee *(see pp67 & 92)*.

⑨ Wickford
MAP E5 ■ **Kayak Centre of Rhode Island: 70 Brown St; 401 295 4400; daily year-round; adm; www.kayakcentre.com**

Artists and craftspeople have flocked to this historic, picturesque village near North Kingstown, and their galleries and shops are big lures for daytrippers. What few visitors realize is that Wickford's location on the west side of Narragansett Bay makes it the ideal launching point for exploring the bay by sea kayak. Inquire about expert guided paddles at the Kayak Centre.

Frosty Drew Observatory, Charlestown

⑩ Charlestown
MAP E5 ■ **Frosty Drew Observatory: 61 Park Ln, Ninigret Park; 401 859 1450; open clear Fri nights; www.frostydrew.org**

It can be hard to tell whether Charlestown is land or water, as the 4-mile (6.5-km) coastline encompasses the largest saltwater marshes in the state. You'll find some of New England's best birding for wading birds and waterfowl in this watery ecosystem between land and sea. Sprawling Ninigret Park has tracks for cyclists and bladers as well as a swimming pool and tennis courts. Every clear Friday night, join the astronomy buffs at Frosty Drew Observatory to scan the skies.

NAVIGATING FROM PROVIDENCE TO NEWPORT

▶ MORNING

Start the day in **Providence** *(see p87)* with a stroll around **Waterplace Park**, a broad pool and amphitheater between Francis and Exchange streets. Cross the Steeple Street Bridge, noting the soaring Ionic columns of the **First Baptist Church in America** on the left. Pop into **Café Choklad** *(2 Thomas St)* for brioche and hot chocolate before entering the **RISD Museum** *(see p42)*, paying special attention to the contemporary art in many different media. The attached store specializes in creations by RISD-affiliated designers.

AFTERNOON

Take I-195 east to Rte 136 south to reach picturesque **Bristol** *(see p88)*. Eat stuffies (stuffed clams) for lunch at **Thames Waterside Bar & Grill** *(251 Thames St)* and see the America's Cup exhibits at the **Herreshoff Marine Museum** *(1 Burnside St)* before continuing south on Rte 114 to **Newport** *(see pp18–19)*. Take a Gilded Age mansion tour of **The Breakers** *(44 Ochre Pt Ave)* and get seats on a sunset cruise in Newport harbor (Bannisters Wharf) aboard a schooner or a motor yacht.

EVENING

Make a night of it at **The Landing** *(30 Bowen's Wharf)*, a large and entertaining waterfront eating and drinking establishment known for its raw bar, live music, and maritime-themed cocktails.

See map on pp86–7

The Best of the Rest

① Audubon Society of Rhode Island Nature Center and Aquarium

MAP F4 ▪ 1401 Hope St, Rte 114, Bristol ▪ 401 949 5454 ▪ Open mid-Apr–mid-Oct: daily; mid-Oct–mid-Apr: call for opening hours ▪ Adm ▪ www.asri.org

Re-discover marine life at this family-friendly wildlife refuge.

② Green Animals Topiary Garden

MAP F5 ▪ 380 Cory's Lane, off Rte 114, Portsmouth ▪ 401 847 1000 ▪ Open late May–early Oct: daily ▪ Adm ▪ www.newportmansions.org

A Rhode Island Red rooster is one of the 80 topiaries at the US's oldest topiary garden, located on a small country estate in Portsmouth.

Green Animals Topiary Garden

③ Beavertail Lighthouse Museum

MAP E5 ▪ Beavertail State Park, Jamestown ▪ 401 423 3270 ▪ Open mid-Jun–early Oct: daily; call for off season hours ▪ Adm ▪ www.beavertaillight.org

There has been a lighthouse on this site since 1749. The keeper's house is now a museum.

④ Casey Farm

MAP E5 ▪ 2325 Boston Neck Rd, Saunderstown (North Kingstown) ▪ 401 295 1030 ▪ Open Jun–mid-Oct: 1–4pm Tue & Thu, 9am–1pm Sat ▪ Adm

Get a glimpse of Rhode Island's agricultural past. Regional farmers' market held on Saturdays.

⑤ The Providence Rink

MAP E4 ▪ 2 Kennedy Plaza, Providence ▪ 401 331 5544 ▪ Open daily ▪ Adm ▪ www.theprovidencerink.com

Skate in the shadow of the state's tallest skyscraper, the 428-ft (130-m) Art Deco "Superman Building."

⑥ Pawtuxet Village

MAP E4 ▪ Warwick

A mid-June parade marks the 1772 burning of a British ship by local patriots. Dozens of Colonial-era buildings feature in the historic district.

⑦ Museum of Work and Culture

MAP E3 ▪ 42 S Main St, Woonsocket ▪ 401 769 9675 ▪ Closed Mon & Sun ▪ Adm ▪ www.rihs.org

This museum in a former textile mill details the lives of those who worked here and in other local factories.

⑧ Gilbert Stuart Birthplace and Museum

MAP E5 ▪ 815 Gilbert Stuart Rd, Saunderstown ▪ 401 294 3001 ▪ Open May–mid-Jun, Sep–mid-Oct: Thu–Mon; mid-Jun–Aug: daily ▪ Adm ▪ www.gilbertstuartmuseum.org

Artist Gilbert Stuart (1755–1828) painted the celebrities of his day. A tour of his birthplace uncovers his modest beginnings.

⑨ East Bay Bike Path

MAP F4

Zip down the bayside path between East Providence and Bristol for views of Narragansett Bay on one side, herons and egrets on the other.

⑩ Tomaquag Museum

MAP E5 ▪ 390a Summit Rd, Exeter ▪ 401 491 9063 ▪ Open 10am–5pm Wed (to 2pm Sat) ▪ Adm ▪ www.tomaquagmuseum.org

This Native American center promotes understanding of Indigenous culture. An expanded new facility is due to open in 2023.

Places to Shop

Colorful display at RISD Store

1 RISD Store
MAP E4 ▪ Chace Center, 30 N Main St, Providence ▪ Closed Mon

Creativity abounds at the RISD Store, the RISD Museum *(see p42)* store, which showcases fashion, furniture, toys, and tools from alumni and faculty members of the school.

2 The Fantastic Umbrella Factory
MAP E5 ▪ 4820 Old Post Rd, Charlestown

No umbrellas are made here and it isn't a factory. It's actually a maze of unusual little shops selling work by local craftsmen and artists, novelty gifts, ethnic treasures, and even pots and plants.

3 Brown & Hopkins Country Store
MAP E4 ▪ 1179 Putnam Pike, Chepachet

Children can select from the "penny candy" counter while their parents browse the home furnishings and accessories at this historic store.

4 Bowen's Wharf
MAP F5 ▪ America's Cup Ave, Newport

Shops on this 18th-century wharf have a nautical flavor. Landlubbers can easily outfit themselves to look like seasoned sailors.

5 Warren
MAP F4

If it's old, you'll probably find it here. A cluster of shops in the compact downtown area of this former whaling port and mill town have turned it into a collector's paradise.

6 Gray's Grist Mill
MAP F5 ▪ Adamsville Rd, Adamsville

For cornmeal to make jonnycakes *(see p65)* at home, stop at this old mill. Visitors may get to see local flint corn ground between immense stones from France.

7 Peter Pots Pottery
MAP E5 ▪ 494 Glen Rock Rd, West Kingston

Collectors favor the modern lines and distinctive glazes of Peter Pots Pottery, founded in 1948. The studio, in an 18th-century mill building, displays the complete line of dinnerware and decorative pieces.

Glazed pot, Peter Pots Pottery

8 Pier Marketplace
MAP E5 ▪ Narragansett Town Beach, Narragansett

On breaks from the beach, sunbathers browse the resort wear and gift shops here, then treat themselves to ice cream or a bag of saltwater taffy.

9 Providence Place
MAP E4 ▪ 1 Providence Place, Providence

This shopping mall in the heart of downtown Providence overlooks Waterfront Park, and has every local and national chain you could ask for.

10 Garden City Center
MAP E4 ▪ Rte 2, Cranston

Established in 1948, this outdoor village-like complex 7 miles (11 km) from Providence offers the same range of shops and dining that you'll find in enclosed malls.

See map on pp86–7

Cafés and Bars

① Perks & Corks
MAP E5 ▪ 48 High St, Westerly

By day, Perks & Corks is a slacker's dream of a coffee bar, with smooth lattes, free Wi-Fi, and enveloping sofas. Then after dark it morphs into a bar serving wines by the glass and killer cocktails.

② Chan's Fine Oriental Dining
MAP E3 ▪ 267 Main St, Woonsocket

Known for its "eggroll jazz," Chan's really hops on the weekends when blues bands and small jazz combos set the diners' fingers snapping. The Chinese fare draws on several regional cuisines.

Outside dining at 22 Bowen's

③ 22 Bowen's Wine Bar and Grille
MAP F5 ▪ 22 Bowen's Wharf, Newport

More than 600 wines make this bar and steakhouse a wine-lover's oasis. Watch boat traffic in the harbor, while tucking into prime rib or slurping down oysters.

④ Fluke Newport
MAP F5 ▪ 41 Bowen's Wharf, Newport

Catch the sunset sitting at this atmospheric bar on Newport Harbor, while enjoying a glass of chardonnay with a bowl of steamed clams.

⑤ Trinity Brewhouse
MAP E4 ▪ 186 Fountain St, Providence

Trinity is a "United Nations" of beer; its ales, lagers, and stout made on the premises recall English, German, and Irish styles. It's a popular after-show venue with playgoers at Trinity Repertory Theatre.

⑥ Olympia Tea Room
MAP E5 ▪ 74 Bay St, Watch Hill

Score one of the outdoor tables at this delightful spot near the Flying Horses Carousel, and you can watch the action while you sip white wine and eat roasted clams with linguine.

⑦ Scales & Shells
MAP F5 ▪ 527 Thames St, Newport

After the dinner rush, this all-fish restaurant turns into a convivial bar where patrons can enjoy local shellfish from the raw bar with a glass of wine or beer.

⑧ George's of Galilee
MAP E5 ▪ 250 Sand Hill Cove Rd, Galilee

Stop off here to savor the pick of the catch from the Galilee fishermen; many spend their evenings at the bar.

⑨ Costantino's Venda Ravioli
MAP E4 ▪ 265 Atwells Ave, Providence

This Italian gourmet shop, with a huge selection of pastas, cheeses, and sausages, also serves coffee and food at tables in the back.

⑩ McKinley's Waterfront
MAP E4 ▪ 1 Division St, East Greenwich

This warm Irish pub is a welcome find on a cool winter night, especially thanks to more than 20 ales on tap. In summer, the outdoor seating overlooking Greenwich Bay is an ideal spot to sip a brew and watch the sailboats go by.

Restaurants

PRICE CATEGORIES

For a three course meal for one with half a bottle of wine (or equivalent meal), taxes and extra charges.

$ under $40 $$ $40–$65 $$$ over $65

1 White Horse Tavern
MAP F5 ▪ 26 Marlborough St, Newport ▪ 401 849 3600 ▪ Closed Sun L; open Sun brunch ▪ $$$

America's oldest tavern, with beamed ceilings, log fires, and candlelit tables, offers classic American cuisine.

2 Le Central
MAP F4 ▪ 483 Hope St, Bristol ▪ 401 396 9965 ▪ Closed Sun–Mon ▪ $$

East Bay (as in Narragansett) meets Left Bank (as in Paris) at this French bistro with a short menu of excellent comfort food (such as cassoulet with duck confit) and great local fish.

3 Trio
MAP E5 ▪ 15 Kingstown Rd, Narragansett ▪ 401 792 4333 ▪ $$

Eat chops, pasta, and seafood at bargain prices or dig into a juicy rib-eye steak or pan-seared scallops.

4 Al Forno
MAP E4 ▪ 577 S Main St, Providence ▪ 401 273 9760 ▪ Closed Tue–Sat L, Sun, Mon ▪ $$$

Al Forno has a great reputation for its tasty baked pastas and meats roasted in a wood-fired oven.

5 Coast in Ocean House
MAP E5 ▪ 1 Bluff Ave, Westerly ▪ 401 584 7000 ▪ Closed Sun L, D Mon–Tue ▪ $$$

This hotel restaurant has an open kitchen

that lets diners watch the chefs prepare elegant seasonal American dishes with creative touches.

6 New Rivers
MAP E4 ▪ 7 Steeple St, Providence ▪ 401 751 0350 ▪ Closed L, Sun D ▪ $$

Spicy contemporary cooking at its best pairs with an intimate dining space for a truly romantic experience.

7 Chez Pascal
MAP E4 ▪ 960 Hope St, Providence ▪ 401 421 4422 ▪ Closed L, Sun ▪ $$

The chef-owner of this unabashedly Burgundian bistro makes his own pâtés, sausages, and confits. Share a charcuterie appetizer then follow it up with the pork of the day.

8 Wright's Farm Restaurant
MAP E4 ▪ 84 Inman Rd, Harrisville ▪ 401 769 2856 ▪ Closed Mon–Fri L, Mon–Wed D ▪ $

This 1,000-seater is the best of the Rhode Island "all-you-can-eat chicken dinner" restaurants.

9 Restaurant 1879, Atlantic Inn
MAP E6 ▪ High St, Block Island ▪ 401 466 5883 ▪ Closed L all year; late Apr–late May & Sep–late Oct Mon–Wed D ▪ $$

Fish and farm produce feature on the menu at this contemporary American eatery. The verandah tables offer spectacular views of the sunset.

10 Matunuck Oyster Bar
MAP F4 ▪ 629 Succotash Rd, Wakefield ▪ 401 783 4202 ▪ $$

The oysters served here are farmed across the street at Potter's Pond, providing a true farm-to-table experience. Fresh scallops and fin fish complete the menu.

Ocean House, perched on a bluff

🔟 Connecticut

The Connecticut River touches four states, but only gives its name to one. Settlers from Boston established Hartford on the riverbank in 1635, ultimately creating the first fully articulated constitution in the American colonies. Three years later, more Bostonians pitched their tents on Long Island Sound and created New Haven, where a small school moved in 1716 and blossomed into Yale University. Harnessing the river for power, Connecticut inventors proved some of the country's most ingenious entrepreneurs. But Connecticut is as beautiful as it is industrious, as American artists demonstrated a century ago when they painted the upland woods and the green and gold marshes of Long Island Sound.

State Capitol, Hartford

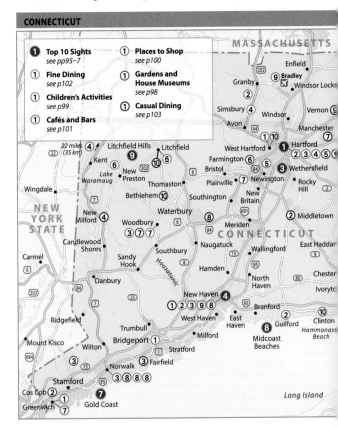

CONNECTICUT

① **Top 10 Sights** see pp95–7	① **Places to Shop** see p100		
① **Fine Dining** see p102	① **Gardens and House Museums** see p98		
① **Children's Activities** see p99			
① **Cafés and Bars** see p101	① **Casual Dining** see p103		

Roses in Elizabeth Park, Hartford

1 Hartford
MAP C4

As the state capital, Hartford has many grand buildings and institutions, from the Victorian-Gothic Connecticut State Capitol in Bushnell Park to the public art museum, Wadsworth Atheneum *(see p41)*, founded in 1842. Hartford was also a hotbed of 19th-century publishing and writing. The Mark Twain House *(see p45)*, where America's greatest yarn-spinner and frontier humorist enjoyed a later life of middle-class comfort, and the Gothic-Revival-style Harriet Beecher Stowe Center *(see p98)* next door underscore the city's literary prominence. Smell the roses – more than 800 varieties of them – in Elizabeth Park, whose rose garden was created in 1904 *(see p98)*.

2 Quiet Corner
MAP D4

The unassuming nickname for Connecticut's northeastern corner suggests that little of excitement has happened here since General Israel Putnam killed the last wolf in the state and made it safe for sheep-farming. In truth, this area of bucolic repose is dotted with the homes of former country squires, including the flamboyant Roseland Cottage Bowen House *(see p98)*. The region is often overlooked, but antiques hunters always stop in Putnam *(see p103)*.

Roseland Cottage, Quiet Corner

3 Wethersfield
MAP C4

The epitome of Colonial and Federal style, the center of Old Wethersfield has a genteel grace that belies its early history as a frontier English community on Native American land. Distinctive architecture lining the community's streets and the weathered headstones of its cemetery make Old Wethersfield a great destination for Colonial history buffs.

Yale University Art Gallery, New Haven

4 New Haven

MAP C5 ▪ Yale Peabody Museum of Natural History: 170 Whitney Ave; 203 432 8987; open 10am–5pm Tue–Sat, noon–5pm Sun; adm; www.peabody.yale.edu

Since the Collegiate School moved to town in 1716, town and gown have been inextricably linked in New Haven. Collections at the Yale University Art Museums (see p42) and the Yale Peabody Museum of Natural History put larger cities to shame. The town's culinary legacy includes the legendary pizzas of Frank Pepe (see p101).

5 New London and Groton

MAP D5

The deepwater port at the mouth of the Thames River – Groton on the east side, New London on the west – lies roughly halfway between Boston and New York. It was a key base of operations for the American Navy during the Revolution; nowadays, ocean cruise ships call here. The massive shipyards of Electric Boat, builder of nuclear-powered submarines, lie in Groton. Explore the Submarine Force Museum (see p42), home of the world's first nuclear-powered sub, the USS *Nautilus*.

AMISTAD AND FREEDOM

In July 1839, enslaved Africans aboard the schooner *Amistad* revolted and were taken into custody at New Haven. Two years of legal battles ensued in New Haven and Hartford, but the enslaved won their freedom. Memorials stand in Connecticut, and a replica ship makes New Haven its home port.

6 Lower Connecticut River

MAP D5 ▪ Connecticut River Museum: 67 Main St, Essex; 860 767 8269; open 10am–5pm Tue–Sun (late May–early Sep daily); adm; www.ctrivermuseum.org

Designated as a "last great place" by the Nature Conservancy, the lower reaches of the Connecticut River, from East Haddam to Lyme, have a magical beauty that captivates artists and sustains fish and wildlife, including large numbers of bald eagles in the winter. See how the American Impressionists captured the scene at the Florence Griswold Museum (see p98) in Old Lyme, and explore the rich history and fascinating ecology of the region at the Connecticut River Museum in Essex.

7 Gold Coast

MAP B6

The communities that lie along the New Haven commuter rail line from Greenwich north to Norwalk are the wealthiest in Connecticut – hence the nickname "Gold Coast." When residents want to shop, they head to Greenwich, where boutiques cater to hedge fund millionaires. To dine or to party, they usually make a beeline for South Norwalk, where a bustling bar and restaurant scene has taken hold.

8 Midcoast Beaches

MAP C6

The great shield of Long Island shelters the sandy shoreline between New Haven Harbor and the mouth of the Connecticut River at Old Lyme (see p48). Protected from storms and erosion, the barrier beaches feature soft sand and gentle surf. Many private beach communities are located here, but so are the

The port of Mystic

main state-owned beaches, which include the 2-mile (3-km) strand at Hammonasset Beach State Park (see p53). Communities like Branford and Clinton live for the sweet but brief summer. Shops are often seasonal.

9 Litchfield Hills

Stretching west from the Connecticut River to the New York border, the Litchfield Hills are Connecticut's proper, manicured mountains. Model 18th- and 19th-century communities of white houses and white churches cluster around tidy town greens. In spring, waterfalls roar off the hillsides and you'll find hardy fishermen wading cold mountain brooks to cast flies for trout. In summer, the smell of newly mown lawns and the sweet scents of perennial flower gardens perfume the air (see pp24–5).

Waterfall, Litchfield Hills

10 Mystic and Stonington
MAP D5, E5

Small seafaring ports of the eastern Connecticut coast, Stonington and Mystic diverged when the latter devel-oped as a tourism center (see p46). Quieter Stonington, 4 miles (6.5 km) away, retains all the hallmarks of a 19th-century fishing and shipping port, and is dotted with upscale boutiques, cheery cafés, and bars where fishermen and antiques dealers drink side by side.

A DRIVING TOUR FROM TALL SHIPS TO SUBMARINES

▶ MORNING

Begin the day by exploring the picturesque fishing and erstwhile shipping village of **Stonington**. Many a tall ship for whaling and overseas trade was constructed along the Mystic River here. To get more of a feel for those maritime days, drive downriver 4 miles (6.5 km) to the village of **Mystic** (which is half in Groton, half in Stonington). Spend the rest of the morning exploring the vessels and the re-created village of **Mystic Seaport** (see p46). Make sure you tour the *Charles W Morgan*, the last surviving wooden whaling ship.

AFTERNOON

Pick up some slices from **Mystic Pizza** (56 W Main St) and follow Rte 1 west through the coastal plain to the **Submarine Force Museum** (see p47). This is where the American nuclear-powered submarine program unfolded after World War II. Tour the first vessel (the USS *Nautilus*) and try your hand at the simulated controls of a complex modern submarine. Just across the Thames River lies the historic town of **New London** (see p96), where you can continue your maritime-themed tour at the **Custom House Maritime Museum** (150 Bank St), which also offers visitors lighthouse tours and boat trips.

Pizza at Mystic Pizza

See map on pp94–5 ←

Gardens and House Museums

1 Roseland Cottage Bowen House

MAP D4 ▪ 556 Rte 169, Woodstock ▪ 860 928 4074 ▪ Open Jun–mid Oct: Wed–Sun ▪ Adm ▪ www.historic newengland.org

This pink, Gothic-style cottage was the summer getaway for the wealthy Bowen family of New York.

Façade of Roseland Cottage

2 Bush-Holley Historic Site

MAP A6 ▪ 39 Strickland Rd, Cos Cob ▪ 203 869 6899 ▪ Open Wed–Sun (Jan–Feb: Sat–Sun) ▪ Adm by guided tour ▪ www.hstg.org

This expanded and modernized site pinpoints two revolutions: the political upheaval of the 1770s and the artistic ferment of American Impressionism, 125 years later.

3 Bartlett Arboretum

MAP A6 ▪ 151 Brookdale Rd, Stamford ▪ 203 322 6971 ▪ Open daily ▪ www.bartlettarboretum.org

Woodlands, wetlands, meadows, and formal gardens make a living museum of 850 specimen trees.

4 Florence Griswold Museum

MAP D5 ▪ 96 Lyme St, Old Lyme ▪ 860 434 5542 ▪ Closed Mon ▪ Adm ▪ www.florencegriswoldmuseum.org

View the history of American Impressionism at this former rooming house, where artist-boarders painted more than 40 panels on the walls.

5 Elizabeth Park Rose Gardens

MAP C4 ▪ Prospect Ave, Hartford ▪ Open daily ▪ www.elizabethparkct.org

In June, plants burst into bloom here, the US's oldest municipal rose garden.

6 Hill-Stead Museum

MAP C4 ▪ 35 Mountain Rd, Farmington ▪ 860 677 4787 ▪ Closed Mon ▪ Adm ▪ www.hillstead.org

This hilltop estate is an aristocratic world of privilege and elegance.

7 Glebe House Museum & Gertrude Jekyll Garden

MAP B5 ▪ 49 Hollow Rd, Woodbury ▪ 203 263 2855 ▪ Open May–Oct: Wed–Sun ▪ Adm ▪ www.glebehouse museum.org

This 1750 home has the only US garden created by famed British designer Gertrude Jekyll.

8 Lockwood-Mathews Mansion Museum

MAP B6 ▪ 295 West Ave, Norwalk ▪ 203 838 9799 ▪ Open Apr–Jan: Wed–Sun ▪ Adm ▪ www.lockwood mathewsmansion.com

Decorative excesses abound at this estate, built for a wealthy banker and railroad tycoon.

9 Harriet Beecher Stowe Center

MAP C4 ▪ 77 Forest St, Hartford ▪ 860 522 9258 ▪ Open daily (Jan–Mar: closed Tue) ▪ Adm ▪ www.harrietbeecherstowecenter.org

Stowe, author of *Uncle Tom's Cabin*, moved here, her last home, in 1873.

10 Bellamy-Ferriday House & Garden

MAP B4 ▪ 9 Main St N, Bethlehem ▪ 203 266 7596 ▪ Open May–Sep: Thu–Sun; Oct: Sat–Sun ▪ Adm ▪ www.ctlandmarks.org

Built for a legendary preacher in the 18th century, the final owner was a civil rights activist.

Children's Activities

1 Connecticut's Beardsley Zoo

MAP B6 ▪ 1875 Noble Ave, Bridgeport ▪ 203 394 6565 ▪ Open daily ▪ Adm ▪ www.beardsleyzoo.org

Siberian tigers are the top cats at this 300-animal zoo. Also spy on the wolves from the observation area.

2 International Skating Center of Connecticut

MAP C4 ▪ 1375 Hopmeadow Dr, Simsbury ▪ 860 651 5400 ▪ Call for public skating hours ▪ Adm ▪ www.isccskate.com

Many Olympic skaters train at this top ice rink that allows public skating.

3 Maritime Aquarium at Norwalk

MAP B6 ▪ 10 N Water St, Norwalk ▪ 203 852 0700 ▪ Open daily ▪ Adm ▪ www.maritimeaquarium.org

This aquatic center highlights the creatures in its own backyard, like harbor seals and sand tiger sharks.

4 Conneticut Science Center

MAP C4 ▪ 250 Columbus Blvd, Hartford ▪ 860 724 3623 ▪ Open daily ▪ Adm

Gripping environmental exhibits dominate this nine-level museum set on Connecticut River banks.

5 Mashantucket Pequot Museum

MAP D5 ▪ 110 Pequot Trail, Mashantucket ▪ 800 411 9671 ▪ Open Apr–Oct: Wed–Sat; Nov: Tue–Sat ▪ Adm ▪ www.pequotmuseum.org

This museum recounts the area's history from the perspective of its pre-colonial inhabitants.

6 Ocean Beach Park

MAP D5 ▪ 98 Neptune Ave, New London ▪ 860 447 3031 ▪ Open late May–early Sep ▪ Adm ▪ www.ocean-beach-park.com

Kids' paradise with a waterslide, beach, miniature golf, and rides.

7 The Dinosaur Place

MAP D5 ▪ 1650 Rte 85, Montville ▪ 860 443 4367 ▪ Park open Apr–Nov, store year-round ▪ Adm ▪ www.thedinosaurplace.com

Every child loves a dinosaur, and over 40 life-sized concrete dinosaurs wait to be discovered here, along nature trails through lush woodlands.

8 Essex Steam Train and Riverboat

MAP D5 ▪ 1 Railroad Ave, Essex ▪ 860 767 0103 or 800 377 3987 ▪ Open May–Oct, Dec ▪ Adm ▪ www.essexsteamtrain.com

Take the throttle in a diesel-train simulator, before riding a vintage train and a riverboat along the Connecticut River.

9 New England Air Museum

MAP C4 ▪ 36 Perimeter Rd, Bradley International Airport, Windsor Locks ▪ 860 623 3305 ▪ Open daily (closed Mon early Sep–late May) ▪ Adm ▪ www.neam.org

Marvel at 65 aircrafts and 200 or so engines that are on display here.

Aircraft, New England Air Museum

10 Children's Museum

MAP C4 ▪ 950 Trout Brook Dr, W Hartford ▪ 860 231 2824 ▪ Open Tue–Sun (Jul–Aug: daily) ▪ Adm ▪ www.thechildrensmuseumct.org

Featuring a planetarium, a wildlife sanctuary, and a wide variety of interactive exhibits, this museum delights and educates kids of all ages.

See map on pp94–5 ←

Places to Shop

1 "The Avenue," Greenwich
MAP A6

Greenwich is the "platinum" town on Connecticut's Gold Coast, and Greenwich Avenue is packed with luxury boutiques that will feather the finest nest.

2 Guilford Art Center
MAP C5 ▪ 411 Church St, Guilford

The town green bustles each July with a juried exhibition of fine crafts. But this center promotes crafts year-round, with classes and a shop full of unique hand-crafted items.

3 Woodbury Pewter
MAP B5 ▪ 860 Main St S, Woodbury

You could well discover the perfect candlestick, bowl, or teapot at a discounted price at the factory outlet of this family-owned company, which was founded in 1952.

4 The Shops at Mohegan Sun
MAP D5 ▪ 1 Mohegan Sun Blvd, Uncasville

Visitors who strike it rich at the gaming tables and slot machines will find plenty to tempt them to splash out on in the upscale shops of this casino complex.

Casino shopping at Mohegan Sun

➔ See map on pp94–5

5 Westfarms Mall, West Hartford
MAP C3 ▪ 500 New Britain Ave, West Hartford

While economic difficulties have taxed more traditional malls in the area, the 160-plus shops and restaurants of the ritzy Westfarms continue to be popular with shoppers seeking everything from high fashion to the newest gadgets.

6 Olde Mistick Village
MAP D5 ▪ Coogan Blvd, Mystic

Lush gardens, a duck pond, and a waterwheel accent this quaint complex not far from Mystic Seaport (see p46).

7 Artisan's Marketplace
MAP C4 ▪ 120 East St, Plainville

More than 400 studio artists working in jewelry, pottery, glass, wood, and fibers display their work here. This shop is housed in a Victorian-style structure with stained-glass windows and fine woodwork.

8 Chapel St, New Haven
MAP C5

Chapel Street skirts the edge of the Yale campus with shops catering to faculty and students alike. Look for designer clothing boutiques and bookstore cafés.

9 Putnam
MAP D4 ▪ Antiques Marketplace: 109 Main St

Setting up the Antiques Marketplace in an ex-department store breathed new life into this former mill town. If you can't find your collectible there, check the town's smaller shops.

10 Clinton Crossing Premium Outlets
MAP C5 ▪ 20-A Killingworth Turnpike, Clinton

Get up to 65 per cent off designer wear at over 70 stores, including Calvin Klein, Kate Spade, Saks Fifth Avenue, and Barneys New York.

Cafés and Bars

Stylish interiors at Max's Oyster Bar

1 Max's Oyster Bar
MAP C4 ■ 964 Farmington Ave, West Hartford ■ 860 236 6299 ■ Closed Sun L; open Sun brunch ■ www.maxrestaurantgroup.com
Showmanlike presentation of the raw-bar offerings sets the tone for this polished, dressy seafood joint.

2 City Steam Brewery Cafe
MAP C4 ■ 942 Main St, Hartford
Great beers brewed on site, super competent waitstaff, and good casual American grub make this restaurant, in a landmark building, a delight. It even has a comedy club.

3 Toad's Place
MAP C5 ■ 300 York St, New Haven
One of the state's biggest dance floors and a sound system that could rock a stadium make Toad's *the* dance venue on a Saturday night.

4 White Hart Provisions
MAP B4 ■ 15 Undermountain Rd, Salisbury ■ www.whitehartinn.com
This small café housed in an old inn doubles up as a grocery store and an espresso bar. The coffee is excellent and there are plenty of breakfast and lunch options to choose from.

5 Water Street Café
MAP E5 ■ 143 Water St, Stonington
Locals favor Water Street for great oysters at the raw bar, chilled white wine, and live guitar music, but don't overlook lively dishes like the lobster spring rolls or warm duck salad.

6 @ the Corner
MAP B4 ■ 3 West St, Litchfield
This hip bakery (formerly The Blue Bakery) makes cakes piled with frosting and pies bursting with fillings. It also serves good coffee and espresso, and a selection of soups, sandwiches, and salads.

7 MacDuff's Public House
MAP A6 ■ 99 Railroad Ave, Greenwich
There's a certain amount of tartan posturing in the decor of this sophisticated Scottish-themed pub. European soccer games often dominate the TV over the bar.

8 Barcelona Wine Bar
MAP B6 ■ 515 West Ave Norwalk
This chic spot offers great Spanish-style tapas, authentic charcuterie, and a list of more than 400 wines.

9 The Cask Republic
MAP C5 ■ 179 Crown St, New Haven
Craft beer is taken seriously here, with more than 40 taps active at a time. The long lists of Scotch and Bourbon are augmented by local crafts spirits. The menu includes charcuterie, burgers, and desserts.

10 Wine Bar at the Griswold Inn
MAP D5 ■ 36 Main St, Essex
Mature cheeses and tapas-style platters can be matched with at least 50 wines at this intimate bar, where maritime art adorns the walls.

Fine Dining

① Oyster Club
MAP D5 ▪ 13 Water St, Mystic ▪ 860 415 9266 ▪ Closed Mon–Thu L ▪ $$$

Restaurant and raw bar that specializes in fresh seafood. The menu showcases the produce of local farmers and fishermen.

② Union League Café
MAP C5 ▪ 1032 Chapel St, New Haven ▪ 203 562 4299 ▪ Closed Sat L, Sun ▪ $$$

The French chef-owner of Union League brings the hearty, market-driven cuisine of a Parisian brasserie to the sophisticated streets of New Haven near Yale University.

③ Max Downtown
MAP C4 ▪ City Place, 185 Asylum St, Hartford ▪ 860 522 2530 ▪ Closed Sat & Sun L ▪ $$$

Tasty beef ranges from petite steak *au poivre* to giant porterhouse at this bustling urban chophouse.

④ Metro Bis
MAP C4 ▪ 4690 Hopmeadow Rd, Simsbury ▪ 860 651 1908 ▪ Closed Sun–Mon & Tue L ▪ $$

The contemporary Metro Bis, set in an elegant mansion, serves fresh, light meals made with local ingredients. Dinner is generally a modestly priced four-course affair. Good wine selection.

⑤ 85 Main
MAP D4 ▪ 85 Main St, Putnam ▪ 860 928 1660 ▪ $$

Sample the superb seafood in either the cozy dining room or the blue-and-white tiled bar.

⑥ Hopkins Inn
MAP B4 ▪ 22 Hopkins Rd, New Preston ▪ 860 868 7295 ▪ Open B, L, D Tue–Sun (Jan–late Mar: Tue–Sat) ▪ $$

The menu is laden with Austrian fare such as schnitzel and sweetbreads. The wine selection follows suit.

⑦ Good News Café
MAP B5 ▪ 694 Main St S, Woodbury ▪ 203 266 4663 ▪ Closed Tue ▪ $$

The chef-owner insists on only local, sustainable, organic products, but her food is never precious, just delicious.

⑧ Match
MAP B6 ▪ 98 Washington St, S Norwalk ▪ 203 852 1088 ▪ Closed L ▪ $$$

Sparkling seafood dishes, inventive seasonal American fare, and rich desserts are a perfect match to the hippest bar on SoNo's restaurant row.

⑨ Todd English's Tuscany
MAP D5 ▪ 1 Mohegan Sun Blvd, Uncasville ▪ 860 862 3236 ▪ $$$

Glitzy environs and expertly executed Northern Italian classics from celebrity chef Todd English.

⑩ Rocks 21 Restaurant
MAP D5 ▪ Inn at Mystic, 3 Williams Ave, Mystic ▪ 860 536 8140 ▪ Closed L Mon–Fri ▪ $$

Classic seafood, wood-fired pizzas, a great raw bar, and craft beer make this waterfront dining room a local favorite. Juicy steaks also help.

View from Rocks 21 Restaurant

Casual Dining

PRICE CATEGORIES

For a three course meal for one with half a bottle of wine (or equivalent meal), taxes and extra charges.

$ under $40 $$ $40–$65 $$$ over $65

① Frank Pepe Pizzeria Napoletana

MAP C5 ▪ 157 Wooster St, New Haven ▪ 203 865 5762 ▪ $

The thin-crust pizza at this no-frills joint open since 1925 has an almost cult following among Yale students. White clam pizza (no tomato sauce) is among the most popular.

② O'Rourke's Diner

MAP C5 ▪ 728 Main St, Middletown ▪ 860 346 6101 ▪ Open 7am–2pm Sun–Thu, 7am–9pm Fri–Sat ▪ $

At this classic diner, dating from the mid-1940s, some of the best food comes fresh off the grill.

③ Rawley's Drive-In

MAP B6 ▪ 1886 Post Rd, Rte 1, Fairfield ▪ 203 259 9023 ▪ Open 11am–6:30pm Mon–Sat ▪ $

When customers stand in line for 20 minutes, it's clear a restaurant is doing something right. It's the hot dogs that keep them coming back for more.

④ The Cookhouse

MAP B5 ▪ 31 Danbury Rd, New Milford ▪ 860 355 4111 ▪ $

Wood-smoked barbecued meat is nearly a religion here. Top sellers are slow-roasted beef brisket, pork back ribs, and Carolina-style pulled pork.

⑤ Captain Scott's Lobster Dock

MAP D5 ▪ 80 Hamilton St, New London ▪ 860 439 1741 ▪ Open Apr–mid-Oct: 11am–9pm daily ▪ Closed mid-Oct–Mar ▪ $

Known for its hot lobster rolls with butter and lobster salad, this seafood shack on a working harbor has an authenticity few can match.

Pizza lovers at Mystic Pizza

⑥ Mystic Pizza

MAP D5 ▪ 56 W Main St, Mystic ▪ 860 536 3700 ▪ $

A Julia Roberts movie made this pizza-and-pasta joint famous, but diners keep returning for the "secret recipe" tomato sauce that's generously slathered on the pizzas.

⑦ Shady Glen

MAP C4 ▪ 840 E Middle Turnpike, Manchester ▪ 860 649 4245 ▪ Open B, L, D daily ▪ $

The homemade ice cream is great, but it's the cheeseburgers that are really the top stars here.

⑧ Blackie's Hot Dog Stand

MAP C5 ▪ 2200 Waterbury Rd, Cheshire ▪ 203 699 1819 ▪ Closed Fri ▪ $

Since 1928, Blackie's has offered hot dogs with or without homemade spicy pepper relish, birch beer on tap, and chocolate milk.

⑨ Rein's

MAP C4 ▪ 435 Hartford Turnpike, Vernon ▪ 860 875 1344 ▪ $

This central Connecticut spot makes better Jewish deli food, including latkes, than most of New York, and is just a quick stop off highway I-84.

⑩ West Street Grill

MAP B4 ▪ 43 West St, Litchfield ▪ 860 567 3885 ▪ $$

Casual lunches are a big hit here, especially the burgers and the pulled short-rib beef sandwich.

See map on pp94–5

ᵀᴼᴾ**10** Vermont

The majestic Green Mountains that cover Vermont compensate for the lack of a seacoast. Between the peaks stand high green meadows and deep, dark lakes, two of which are said to harbor sea serpents. Settled in the 1700s under conflicting land grants from New York and New Hampshire, Vermont was an independent republic from 1777, becoming the 14th US state in 1791. A rugged independence persists in Vermonters, who despite severe winter weather seem to be outdoors year-round, hiking, skiing, skating, sledding, cycling, kayaking, hunting, and fishing, sometimes against a brilliant background of fall leaves.

Skiing in Northeast Kingdom

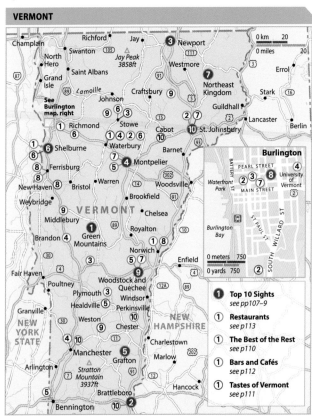

VERMONT

① **Top 10 Sights**
see pp107–9

① **Restaurants**
see p113

① **The Best of the Rest**
see p110

① **Bars and Cafés**
see p112

① **Tastes of Vermont**
see p111

The breathtaking wilderness of the beautiful Green Mountains

1 Green Mountains

It would scarcely be an exaggeration to say that Vermont *is* the Green Mountains (see pp26–7) and vice versa, as this ancient range in the Appalachian chain touches almost every part of the state.

2 Brattleboro
MAP K6

Vermont's first permanent English settlement, Brattleboro flourished in the 19th century as a Connecticut River manufacturing town at the juncture of Vermont, Massachusetts, and New Hampshire. The town got a new lease on life in the 1960s as the counterculture capital of the upper Connecticut River Valley, and is known around the state for its stridently liberal politics. The thriving cultural community includes several galleries, a performing arts center, and a school of circus arts that is open to the general public.

3 Newport
MAP L5

Vermont's northernmost city is set at the southern edge of Lake Memphremagog, a body of water 27 miles (43 km) long that is shared with the province of Quebec. A glacial lake that was a saltwater inland sea at the end of the Laurentian glaciation, Memphremagog has long been rumored to hold a sea serpent akin to the Loch Ness Monster. Sightings of the elusive creature that locals call "Memphre" date to the 18th century. Take a stroll along the attractive waterfront and see if you can spy those watery coils from the safety of the shore.

4 Montpelier
MAP K3

For an iconic Vermont image, stop along State Street during foliage season to take a picture with the gold-domed State House backed by a hillside of red and flame-orange maple trees. The city was selected for state capital in 1805 because it lies at the geographic center of Vermont as well as in the main east-west pass through the Green Mountains. Today Montpelier has a thriving home-grown acoustic music and a dining scene reliant on local farm products.

Vermont State House, Montpelier

5 Grafton
MAP K6 ■ **Plummer's Sugar House:** 2866 Townshend Rd; 802 843 2207; www.plummerssugarhouse.com ■ **MKT Wine & Cheese:** 162 Main St; 802 843 2255; www.mktgrafton.com ■ **Old Tavern:** 92 Main St; 802 843 2248

Wealthy philanthropists saved this beautiful village in the 1960s by forming the Windham Foundation to restore its handsome buildings and revitalize commerce. Visit Plummer's Sugar House, purchase Grafton Village Cheese, or enjoy a meal at the 200-year-old Old Tavern.

Verdant pastures of Shelburne Farms

6 Shelburne
MAP J3 ■ **Vermont Wildflower Farm:** open Mon–Sat; 170 Boyer Cir, Williston; 802 425 3641; www.vermontwildflowerfarm.com

Standing on high banks above Lake Champlain just south of Burlington, Shelburne is a village of magnificent dairy farms, not least among them the historic spread of Shelburne Farms (see p111). A locomotive, a steamship, and buildings crammed with folk art dot the rolling meadows of Shelburne Museum (see p41).

The Vermont Wildflower Farm has relocated to Williston, near Shelburne, and showcases over 350 species of flowering plants and trees.

7 Northeast Kingdom
MAP L2

"Northeast Kingdom" refers to Essex, Orleans, and Caledonia counties in the state's northeast corner – an area sometimes referred to simply as "The Kingdom." In Vermont cultural shorthand, the term connotes both a rural, frontier toughness and an easy familiarity with the latest developments in the world of avant-garde performance art. With only two large communities, St. Johnsbury and Newport, it is one of the most rural parts of the state. The Northeast Kingdom is known above all for skiing, resplendent autumn foliage, and maple syrup.

8 Burlington
MAP J3

Settled shortly before the American Revolution, Burlington, unlike the rest of Vermont, takes its identity less from the Green Mountains than from the great inland sea of Lake Champlain. Burlington shipyards turned the mountain timber into trading vessels. Visitors can learn about the region's history on the Lake Champlain Cruise (see p60). Blessed with a handsome, largely 19th-century downtown, Burlington also enjoys a busy cultural life as a by-product of the presence of the state university.

Marketplace, downtown Burlington

Traditional houses, Woodstock

9 Woodstock and Quechee
MAP K5

It's little wonder that Woodstock is such a popular destination for weddings. With its broad town green, meticulously restored Federal and Victorian houses, covered bridge in the middle of town, and five churches boasting Paul Revere bells, it is the very picture of old-time Vermont. Even the Billings Farm (see p38) serves as a museum of Vermont rural life. Head east on Route 4 to see the vertigo-inspiring 165-ft (50-m) deep gorge carved by the Ottauquechee River.

10 St. Johnsbury
MAP L3 ■ Athenaeum Gallery: 1171 Main St; 802 748 8291; open 10am–5:30pm Mon, Wed & Fri, noon–7pm Tue & Thu, 10am–3pm Sat; www.stjathenaeum.org

"St. J," as Vermonters call it, is both the hub of the state's Northeast Kingdom and the gateway between Vermont's Green Mountains and New Hampshire's White Mountains. When Thaddeus Fairbanks invented the platform scale in 1830, the town became his manufacturing center. The Fairbanks clan left its stamp on St. Johnsbury, donating both the Fairbanks Museum & Planetarium (see p110), and the Athenaeum, a library and gallery with magnificent landscape paintings.

A DAY IN ROBERT FROST COUNTRY

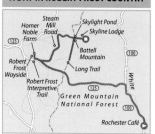

▶ MORNING

Robert Frost (1874–1963), the seminal poet of the New England countryside, spent 39 summers near the **Green Mountain National Forest** (see pp26–7). This easy-to-moderate day of hiking captures the poet and the landscape he loved. Start with pancakes and maple syrup at the **Rochester Café** (Rte 100, Rochester; 802 767 4302), at the same soda fountain where Frost used to eat, and have the café pack you a lunch. Drive west on Rte 125 to the **Robert Frost Interpretive Trail**, where you can read some of Frost's pithy verse and learn to identify native plants. Just east of the almost adjacent **Robert Frost Wayside** picnic area, a 5-minute walk on an unmarked dirt road will bring you to Frost's cabin at the **Homer Noble Farm**, maintained as he left it.

AFTERNOON

When the muse evaded Frost, he sought solace in the woods. For a hike, drive east on Rte 125 a short distance and turn left onto **Steam Mill Road**. A bit further on, park at the **Skylight Pond** trailhead. The path ascends the flank of **Battell Mountain**, crisscrossing the hillside through a forest of white birch, red oak, and hemlocks. Overgrown and tumbledown stone walls proclaim old boundary lines, as forest reclaims farmland. The moderate 45-minute climb ends on a ridge connecting to the legendary **Long Trail**. Turn left for a short hike to **Skyline Lodge**, a rustic shelter for hikers.

See map on p106 ←

The Best of the Rest

Enthralled child, Montshire Museum

① Montshire Museum
MAP L4 ▪ 1 Montshire Rd, Norwich ▪ 802 649 2200 ▪ Open daily ▪ Adm ▪ www.montshire.org

This museum has outdoor trails and science exhibits that delight children.

② Fairbanks Museum & Planetarium
MAP L3 ▪ 1302 Main St, St. Johnsbury ▪ 802 748 2372 ▪ Open daily ▪ Closed Jan ▪ Adm ▪ www.fairbanksmuseum.org

Vermont flora and fauna mingle with Philippine and Indian birds in this natural history museum.

③ President Calvin Coolidge State Historic Site
MAP K5 ▪ 3780 Rte 100 A, Plymouth ▪ 802 672 3773 ▪ Open daily late May–mid-Oct ▪ Adm ▪ www.historicsites.vermont.gov

The independent spirit of his home village inspired Coolidge (1872–1933). Today, much remains the same.

④ Robert Hull Fleming Museum
MAP J3 ▪ 61 Colchester Ave, Burlington ▪ 802 656 2090 ▪ Closed Mon; mid-Dec–mid-Jan; mid-Mar; Jul–Aug ▪ Adm ▪ www.uvm.edu/~fleming

Artifacts ranging from African masks and pre-Columbian pottery to medieval manuscripts and Andy Warhol prints are displayed here.

⑤ Bennington Museum & Grandma Moses Gallery
MAP J6 ▪ 75 Main St, Bennington ▪ 802 447 1571 ▪ Closed Jan; Feb–May, Nov & Dec: Wed ▪ Adm ▪ www.benningtonmuseum.org

Stop by and browse this major collection of work by folk artist Grandma Moses (1860–1961).

⑥ VTSSM
MAP K3 ▪ 1 S Main St, Stowe ▪ 802 253 9911 ▪ Closed Mon–Tue ▪ Donation ▪ www.vtssm.com

Vermont Ski and Snowboard Museum charts skiing in the state from the introduction of powered lifts in the 1930s to the present day.

⑦ Vermont Institute of Natural Science
MAP K5 ▪ 149 Natures Way (off Rte 4), Quechee ▪ 802 359 5000 ▪ Adm ▪ www.vinsweb.org

Injured eagles, hawks, and other raptors, unable to return to the wild, get a second home here.

⑧ Rokeby Museum
MAP J3 ▪ 334 US-7, Ferrisburgh ▪ 802 377 3406 ▪ Open mid-May–late Oct: daily ▪ Adm ▪ www.rokeby.org

This farm (now a museum) played a key role in the Underground Railroad.

⑨ Bread and Puppet Museum
MAP L6 ▪ R753 Heights Rd, Glover ▪ 802 525 3031 ▪ Open Jun–Oct: daily ▪ Adm ▪ www.breadandpuppet.org/museum

Browse the huge collection of puppets, masks, and props of the legendary radical agitprop street theater company.

⑩ American Museum of Fly Fishing
MAP K6 ▪ 4070 Main St, Manchester ▪ 802 362 3300 ▪ Closed Sun–Mon ▪ Adm ▪ www.amff.com

Exhibits such as rods, reels, and flies tell the story of fly fishing.

Tastes of Vermont

1 Cold Hollow Cider Mill
MAP K3 ■ 3600 Waterbury-Stowe Rd, Rte 100, Waterbury Center ■ Open daily ■ www.coldhollow.com
Drop by for freshly pressed cider. The store brims with Vermont specialties.

2 Lake Champlain Chocolates
MAP J3 ■ 750 Pine St, Burlington ■ Open daily ■ www.lakechamplainchocolates.com
The flagship store of the decadent chocolate brand features a giant collection of chocolate sculptures.

3 The Alchemist Brewery
MAP K3 ■ 100 Cottage Club Rd, Stowe ■ Open daily ■ www.alchemistbeer.com
Specializing in unfiltered IPAs, this brewery attracts a loyal fanbase to its beer garden.

4 Ben & Jerry's Ice Cream Factory
MAP K3 ■ Rte 100, Waterbury ■ 866 BJ TOURS ■ Open daily ■ Adm ■ www.benjerry.com
Vermont farms provide the rich milk for the super-premium ice creams and yogurts that are made here.

5 Crowley Cheese Co
MAP K5 ■ 14 Crowley Ln, Healdville ■ Open Mon–Sat ■ www.crowleycheese.com
This is Vermont's oldest cheese factory (1882), noted for its prize-winning Colby cheese.

6 Shelburne Farms
MAP J3 ■ 1611 Harbor Rd, Shelburne ■ Store open daily; tours May–Oct ■ Adm for tours ■ www.shelburnefarms.org
Milk from Brown Swiss cows is turned into cheddar at this farm overlooking Lake Champlain.

7 Maple Grove Farms Maple Museum and Gift Shop
MAP L3 ■ 1052 Portland St, St. Johnsbury ■ Open Apr–May: Mon–Fri; Jun–Dec: daily ■ Adm ■ www.maplegrove.com
Learn how tree sap becomes a breakfast favorite as well as iconic tooth-tingling maple leaf candies.

8 Lincoln Peak Winery
MAP J4 ■ 142 River Rd, New Haven ■ Open late May–mid-Oct: 11am–5pm daily; mid-Oct–Dec: Wed–Sun; Jan–late May: Fri–Sun ■ www.lincolnpeakvineyard.com
The tasting room at Lincoln Peak offers some of the best wines made in the inhospitable northerly climate.

Chocolates at Lake Champlain

9 Vermont Country Store
MAP K5 ■ 657 Main St, Weston ■ Open daily ■ www.vermontcountrystore.com
This emporium still has a pickle barrel and huge wedges of cheddar. Try its own Vermont Common Crackers.

10 Farmers' Store
MAP L3 ■ 2878 Main St, Cabot ■ Closed Jan–late May: Sun ■ www.cabotcheese.com
Vermont's largest cheese producer stocks a wide range of dairy products.

Dairy items for sale, Farmers' Store

See map on p106

Bars and Cafés

1 Higher Ground
MAP J3 ▪ 1214 Williston Rd, Burlington ▪ 802 253 4364 ▪ $

The state's premier music venue hosts an array of acts, ranging from chart-toppers to obscure indie bands. Three full-service bars keep the crowds fueled.

2 Drink
MAP J3 ▪ 135 St. Paul St, Burlington ▪ $

This sophisticated northern Vermont bar offers splashy mojitos, cosmopolitans, and a selection of home-infused vodkas. Traditionalists may bypass the stylish lounge in favor of beer and televised sports at the bar.

3 McGrath's Irish Pub
MAP K5 ▪ Inn at Long Trail, 709 Rte 4, Sherburne Pass, Killington ▪ $

Darts, Guinness on draft, and live music on weekends await the loyal following at this amiable pub.

Elegant interior of The Silver Fork

4 The Silver Fork
MAP K6 ▪ 48 West Rd, Manchester Village ▪ $

Housed in a former village library, this stylish café serves international fare with French and Caribbean flavors.

5 Three Penny Taproom
MAP K3 ▪ 108 Main St, Montpelier ▪ $

Home of the craft beer movement in Vermont, this cool bar also serves simple bistro fare at bargain prices.

6 Prohibition Pig
MAP K3 ▪ 23 S Main St, Waterbury ▪ $

A friendly local hangout that whips up classic cocktails alongside Vermont's most acclaimed craft beers. Delicious barbecue fare and a gluten-free menu keep the patrons satisfied.

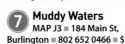
Prohibition Pig

7 Muddy Waters
MAP J3 ▪ 184 Main St, Burlington ▪ 802 652 0466 ▪ $

A venerable coffee house with outstanding expresso, local bagels and pastries, and live music in the evenings.

8 Jasper Murdock's Alehouse
MAP L4 ▪ 325 Main St, Norwich ▪ $

This cozy pub brews its own English-style ales. It attracts large numbers of students from nearby Dartmouth College, as well as local ski buffs.

9 Matterhorn
MAP K3 ▪ 4969 Mountain Rd, Stowe ▪ $

The first bar south of Mount Mansfield is the perfect party stop after a day of skiing. Sushi dominates the menu, but the burgers are good too.

10 Mocha Joe's Café
MAP K6 ▪ 82 Main St, Brattleboro ▪ $

Artists, musicians, and all self-respecting Brattleboro Bohemians get caffeinated at this roaster café known for its winter maple lattes and summer limeade.

Restaurants

PRICE CATEGORIES
For a three course meal for one with half
a bottle of wine (or equivalent meal),
taxes and extra charges.

$ under $40 $$ $40–$65 $$$ over $65

① Inn at Shelburne Farms Restaurant

MAP J3 ▪ 1611 Harbor Rd, Shelburne
▪ 802 985 8498 ▪ Open mid-May–
mid-Oct, B and D daily, Sun brunch
▪ $$$

This elegant dining room makes the
most of northern Vermont's short
but high-grade harvest, from early
lettuces to fall apples.

② Hen of the Wood

MAP K3 ▪ 92 Stowe St,
Waterbury ▪ 802 244 7300 ▪ Closed L,
Sun–Mon ▪ $$

Plates here embody the essence of
gastronomic Vermont: local meats,
seasonal farm vegetables, foraged
foods, and exquisite cheeses.

③ Farmhouse Tap & Grill

MAP J3 ▪ 160 Bank St,
Burlington ▪ 802 859 0888
▪ Open L & D daily ▪ $$

Gourmet burgers, craft beer, and
dinner plates laden with Vermont
farm produce make Farmhouse a
local favorite.

④ Cafe Provence

MAP K4 ▪ 111 Center St,
Brandon ▪ 802 247 9997 ▪ Closed
Mon ▪ $$

The Provençal chef uses Vermont
produce to create authentic country
French food served in an intimate
village bistro.

⑤ The Mill at Simon Pearce

MAP K5 ▪ 1760 Quechee Main St,
Quechee ▪ 802 295 1470 ▪ Closed
Sun L; open Sun brunch ▪ $$$

Savor the riverside location, superb
food, and fine wine. Pearce, a famed
glass artist, has a studio on site.

⑥ Kitchen Table Bistro

MAP K3 ▪ 1840 W Main St,
Richmond ▪ 802 434 8686 ▪ Closed L,
Sun & Mon D ▪ $$

This cozy bistro has a strong
northern-French accent. Try
the maple-smoked pork and
braised kale.

⑦ Oakes and Evelyn

MAP K3 ▪ 52 Main St,
Montpelier ▪ 802 347 9100
▪ Closed Mon & Tue ▪ $

The contemporary farm-to-table
menu here has an array of
vegetarian dishes.

A cauliflower dish, Oakes and Evelyn

⑧ Starry Night Café

MAP J3 ▪ 5371 Rte 7,
Ferrisburgh ▪ 802 877 6316 ▪ Closed
L, Mon & Tue D ▪ $$

Dining here in a covered bridge or a
former cider house is as magical as
the restaurant name. Hearty American
food is mostly raised or grown locally.

⑨ American Flatbread

MAP J4 ▪ 137 Maple St,
Middlebury ▪ 802 388 3300 ▪ Closed
L, Sun–Thu; D, Sun–Mon ▪ $

This wildly popular eatery churns out
gourmet pizzas and salads made with
organic, Vermont-raised ingredients.

⑩ The Inn at Weathersfield

MAP K5 ▪ 1342 Rte 106,
Perkinsville ▪ 802 263 9217 ▪ Closed
L, Mon–Wed D ▪ $$

Inventive chefs here might pair pork
loin and scallops with capers, or
pumpkin soup with local blue cheese.

See map on p106

TOP 10 New Hampshire

The aptly nicknamed Granite State is a thick wedge of rock between two great rivers – the Connecticut on the west and the Piscataqua on the east. Its initial settlements in the 1620s were strictly coastal, but within a generation, explorers had ventured deep into its woods for furs and timber. Despite the rugged topography, many of the villages in the White Mountains were well established by the time of the American Revolution. Most residents live along the southern edge of the state, often driving down to Massachusetts for employment. Northern New Hampshire remains almost untracked forest. American scenic tourism began in the White Mountains in the 1820s, and those peaks and the villages on their flanks remain major vacation destinations. New Hampshire also boasts a chain of alpine lakes and a lively seacoast, where vacationers from as far away as Montreal flock to the shore.

The church in Keene

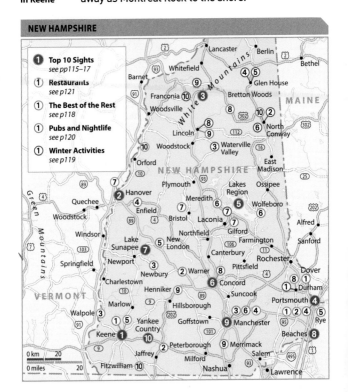

NEW HAMPSHIRE

1 **Top 10 Sights**
   see pp115–17

1 **Restaurants**
   see p121

1 **The Best of the Rest**
   see p118

1 **Pubs and Nightlife**
   see p120

1 **Winter Activities**
   see p119

1 Keene
MAP L6

At 132 ft (40 m) wide for most of its length, Keene's attractive Main Street is easily the widest in New England. This shire town has a lively mix of old-time shops and art galleries, as well as the good bars and cafés you'd expect in a college community. At its heart stands the pretty United Church of Christ with its soaring white steeple.

2 Hanover
MAP L4 ■ Ledyard Canoe Club of DOC: Ledyard Bridge; 603 643 0709; open May–Oct; call for availability; adm

It's hardly a bad thing, but Dartmouth College utterly overwhelms the rest of Hanover. The town green and the college green are one and the same, and the shopping district clearly favors the tastes of young scholars and their well-heeled parents. But Dartmouth holds many riches, even for the visitor just passing through. Not least among them are the art treasures of the recently expanded Hood Museum of Art (see p43). Hanover sits on the Connecticut River and is popular with canoeists. Most recreational programs of the Dartmouth Outing Club, including boat rentals, are open to non-students as well.

3 White Mountains
The White Mountains (see pp20–21) have a special place in American history. When early

White Mountains, a hub for hikers

19th-century poets, philosophers, and theologians sought inspiration, they made a pilgrimage to these majestic hills to experience the sublime rising peaks and plunging glens.

4 Portsmouth
MAP N6

Portsmouth was New Hampshire's first English community, settled at the mouth of the Piscataqua River in 1623. Plentiful timber and a deep harbor made it a natural for ship-building, and from 1780 to 1870 its merchant traders grew rich. Walk through the handsome squares of the Colonial settlement to see some of New England's finest town mansions, and to breathe the salt air that has always been Portsmouth's life-blood. The historic houses and period furnishings of Strawbery Banke (see p38) relate the city's four-century domestic history.

Portsmouth, on the Piscataqua River

Small islands dotting the water in New Hampshire's Lakes Region

5 Lakes Region

Vast lakes and small ponds form a stunning watery belt *(see pp30–31)* across New Hampshire's midriff. Seek solitude among the loons on a remote cove, or party all night on Weirs Beach.

6 Concord

MAP M5 ▪ **New Hampshire Historical Society: 30 Park St; 603 228 6688; open 9:30am–5pm Tue–Sat, noon–5pm Sun; adm; www.nh history.org**

The state capital Concord is a serene little town steeped in history. Its handsome 1819 State House is one of the country's oldest. The celebrated Concord stagecoaches that helped to open up the American West were manufactured here; Mark Twain memorably described one as being "like a cradle on wheels." The city's most famous modern resident was schoolteacher Christa McAuliffe (1948–86), who died aboard the *Challenger* space shuttle. Her dedication to science education is honored at the McAuliffe-Shepard Discovery Center *(see p62)*.

State House, Concord

7 Lake Sunapee

MAP L5 ▪ **Sunapee Cruises: 1 Lake Ave, Sunapee; 603 938 6465; open late May–mid-Oct; adm; www.sunapeecruises.com**

This alpine lake – whose name, meaning "wild goose waters," is of American-Indian origin – was a Victorian resort where vacationers stepped off the train onto steamboats to be delivered to their grand lakefront hotels. The hotels are gone, but private cottages ring the lake, and the harbors of Sunapee and Newbury are busy spots in the summer, with free outdoor concerts and bustling restaurants. Take a scenic cruise on the lake, or have a dinner cruise on a steamboat.

8 Beaches

MAP N6

New Hampshire's brief stretch of coastline is more rock than sand, with rugged promontories and rock jetties protecting its fishing harbors. The coast is also punctuated by swaths of coarse brown sand. Jenness State Beach and Wallis Sands State Beach in Rye, and North Beach in Hampton, have the best-maintained facilities and gentlest swimming. Hampton Beach *(see p52)* is by far the most popular.

9 Manchester

MAP M6

The largest city in northern New England, Manchester rose and fell with the Amoskeag Mill. From humble beginnings in 1809 on the east bank of the Merrimack River, the

LIVE FREE OR DIE

Some visitors might imagine that the state motto proclaimed on license plates refers to New Hampshire's lack of sales and income taxes. In fact it originated with a toast that the state's Revolutionary War hero, General John Stark, gave by letter to the 1809 reunion of veterans of the Battle of Bennington, when poor health prevented him from attending: "Live free or die: death is not the worst of evils."

town grew into the world's largest cotton-mill complex by the dawn of the 20th century. The textile era has long since ended here, but the hulking brick mills have been transformed into a complex of restaurants, college classrooms, offices, and apartments. The city's comprehensive Currier Museum of Art (see p40) is the state's premier art museum.

Peterborough, stunning in the fall

⑩ Yankee Country
MAP L6

Yankee Publishing, which produces both *Yankee Magazine* and the *Old Farmer's Almanac*, is based in Dublin. The homespun village and its neighboring towns of Peterborough and Jaffrey epitomize the gentle New England countryside. The region was a popular resort area in the late 19th century, and all three villages have long served as staging grounds for people preparing to climb nearby Mount Monadnock (see p55), said to be the second most-climbed peak in the world after Japan's Mount Fuji.

A DAY'S DRIVE ON THE KANCAMAGUS HIGHWAY

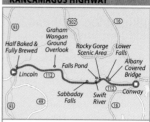

▶ MORNING

Before you begin the 35-mile (56-km) drive from **Lincoln** to **Conway** (see pp20–21), stop at **Half Baked & Fully Brewed** (187 Main St, Lincoln) for picnic fixings. After a gentle 11-mile (18-km) rise, you'll climb through steep switchbacks for 4 miles (6 km) to the **Graham Wangan Ground Overlook** for jaw-dropping mountain views. As the road twists and turns for another 6 miles (10 km), watch for a right turn into the trailhead to **Sabbaday Falls**. A short walk through dense, pine-scented woods brings you to the waterfall, which makes a wonderfully dramatic 90-degree dogleg as it tumbles down a mountain. The **Rocky Gorge Scenic Area**, a further 4 miles (6 km) east, is a geological wonder. Cross a bridge to follow a short trail to **Falls Pond**, where fishermen cast for trout.

AFTERNOON

Another 3 miles (5 km) east, spread your food on a picnic table at **Lower Falls**, overlooking the boulder-strewn **Swift River**. The green pools below the largest boulders make cool summer swimming holes. In the fall, photographers scramble across the boulders trying to capture the intense red and yellow foliage. From the Falls, it's only a short drive to the Albany Covered Bridge. The weathered 120-ft (37-m) span is a favorite with photographers and you'll surely want a shot to remember your journey. From the bridge, it's about 7 fairly flat miles (11 km) to the end of the "Kanc" in **Conway**.

See map on p114

The Best of the Rest

1 Children's Museum of New Hampshire

MAP N5 ▪ 6 Washington St, Dover ▪ 603 742 2002 ▪ Closed Mon except in summer and school vacations ▪ Adm ▪ www.childrens-museum.org

A yellow submarine and an interactive sound sculpture are two of the imaginative exhibits here.

2 Mount Kearsarge Indian Museum

MAP L5 ▪ 18 Highlawn Rd, Warner ▪ 603 456 2600 ▪ Open May–Oct: daily ▪ Adm ▪ www. indianmuseum.org

Exhibit, Mount Kearsage Indian Museum

Admire intricate craftwork and learn how plants were used for food and medicine at this fascinating museum.

3 Mount Sunapee State Park

MAP L5 ▪ 86 Beach Access Rd, Newbury ▪ 603 763 5561 (park); 603 763 3500 (ski resort) ▪ Open late May–mid-Sep (beach); late Nov–mid-Apr (ski resort) ▪ Adm ▪ www.nhstateparks.org

This state park has a pristine lake for swimming and boating, as well as trails for hiking and skiing.

4 Enfield Shaker Museum

MAP L5 ▪ 447 Rte 4A, Enfield ▪ 603 632 4346 ▪ Open Jun–Dec ▪ Adm ▪ www.shakermuseum.org

Like the furniture and tools displayed inside, the Great Stone Dwelling has an austere grace.

Enfield Shaker Museum

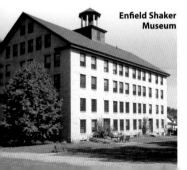

5 Odiorne Point State Park

MAP N6 ▪ Rte 1A, Rye ▪ 603 436 7406 ▪ Open year-round daily ▪ Adm ▪ www.nhstateparks.org

Tidal pools, pebble beaches, and marshlands surround the site of the state's first English settlement.

6 Wright Museum

MAP M5 ▪ 77 Center St, Wolfeboro ▪ 603 569 1212 ▪ Open May–Oct ▪ Adm ▪ www.wrightmuseum.org

This museum highlights the World War II efforts of US services and their home-front sacrifices.

7 Wellington State Park

MAP L5 ▪ 614 W Shore Rd, Bristol ▪ 603 744 2197 ▪ Open daily ▪ Adm ▪ www.nhstateparks.org

The swimming beach on Newfound Lake is a summer favorite. Hike the nature trails in the fall for the foliage.

8 Crawford Notch State Park

MAP M4 ▪ 1464 Rte 302, Hart's Location ▪ 603 374 2272 ▪ Open daily ▪ Adm ▪ www.nhstateparks.org

This vast wilderness is a hiker's paradise. Climb 2,804-ft (855-m) Mount Willard for great views.

9 Budweiser Brewery Experience

MAP M6 ▪ 221 Daniel Webster Hwy, Merrimack ▪ 603 595 1202 ▪ Hours vary, check website ▪ www.budweisertours.com

This informative brewery tour concludes with a tasting for over 21s.

10 Rhododendron State Park

MAP L6 ▪ 424 Rockwood Pond Rd, Fitzwilliam ▪ 603 532 8862 ▪ Open year-round ▪ www.nhstateparks.org

Immerse yourself in the color and aroma of the towering rhododendrons that bloom here in July.

Winter Activities

① UNH Wildcats Hockey
MAP N5 ▪ Whittemore Arena, 128 Main St, Durham ▪ 603 862 4057 ▪ Open Oct–Apr ▪ Adm ▪ www.unhwildcats.com

A family-friendly atmosphere underscores the games of this powerhouse college Division I hockey team.

② Outdoor Skating
MAP M4 ▪ Schouler Park, Main St, North Conway ▪ Open Dec–Mar

Low temperatures guarantee a long season of outdoor skating at Schouler Park rink in this picturesque village.

③ Nordic Skiing
MAP M4 ▪ Waterville Valley Resort, 1 Ski Area Rd, Waterville Valley ▪ 603 236 4666 ▪ Open Dec–Mar ▪ Adm ▪ www.waterville.com

Glide along scenic trails at the edge of the White Mountain National Forest.

④ SnowCoach
MAP M3 ▪ Great Glen Trails, 1 Mt Washington Auto Rd, Gorham ▪ 603 466 3988 ▪ Open Dec–Mar: daily ▪ Adm ▪ www.mtwashington autoroad.com

This special vehicle carries passengers above the treeline on Mt Washington Auto Road for winter vistas.

⑤ Snow Tubing
MAP M3 ▪ Great Glen Trails, 1 Mt Washington Auto Rd, Gorham ▪ 603 466 3988 ▪ Open Dec–Mar: daily ▪ Adm ▪ www.greatglentrails.com

Climb a snow-covered hill and then whiz back down on a cushy inner tube.

⑥ Ice Climbing
MAP M4 ▪ Eastern Mountain Sports School, 2686 White Mountain Hwy, North Conway ▪ 845 668 2030 ▪ Open Dec–Mar: daily ▪ Adm ▪ www.ems.com

Learn to climb in ice and snow with crampons, picks, ropes, and harnesses. Face the ultimate adventure in an ascent of Mount Washington.

⑦ Snowshoeing
MAP M5 ▪ Prescott Farm Environmental Education Center: 928 White Oaks Rd, Laconia; 603 366 5695; open daily; www.prescottfarm.org

A popular winter sport, snowshoeing involves walking on snow wearing specialized snowshoes. Prescott Farm has over 3 miles (5 km) of woodland, pond, and field trails for snowshoeing. Modest fee for snowshoe rental.

⑧ Snowmobiling
MAP L4 ▪ SledVentures, 514 US Rte 3, Lincoln ▪ 603 238 2571 ▪ Open Nov–Mar ▪ Adm ▪ www.nhsledventures.com

Marvel at the hushed beauty of New Hampshire's snow-clad mountains in winter on a guided snowmobile tour.

Snowmobiling in the mountains

⑨ Alpine Skiing
MAP L/M 3–4

Thanks to the White Mountains, New Hampshire has a multitude of top-class alpine ski runs and all are easily reached via Rte 16 or I-91.

⑩ New England Ski Museum
MAP L3 ▪ Exit 34B I-93/Franconia Notch Parkway, Franconia ▪ 603 823 7177 ▪ Open late May–Mar: daily ▪ www.skimuseum.org

The first aerial ski tramway in the US opened on Cannon Mountain in 1938. This is therefore a fitting location for this ski museum that traces the development of the sport from its roots to more modern times.

See map on p114

Pubs and Nightlife

 Elm City Brewing
MAP L6 ■ Colony Mill Marketplace, 222 West St, Keene
The four-beer sampler offers a taste of the ales, porters, and stouts brewed in this 19th-century former woolen mill. Cozy booths make it ideal for conversation.

 Harlow's Pub
MAP L6 ■ 3 School St, Peterborough
Visit this relaxed venue on Thursday nights for a bluegrass jam; or try weekends, when it might be rock and blues, reggae, or even gypsy jazz.

③ Strange Brew Tavern
MAP M6 ■ 88 Market St, Manchester
This friendly, bustling tavern serves a wide range of local brews along with an extensive menu of familiar pub grub. Local bands perform most nights.

④ The Press Room
MAP N6 ■ 77 Daniel St, Portsmouth
Still going strong after three decades, this pub features live jazz from Sunday to Tuesday. The rest of the week might bring Celtic music and sea shanties, blues, soul, folk, or even poetry.

 Flying Goose Brew Pub
MAP L5 ■ 40 Andover Rd, New London
With a schedule of live music, "the Goose" lures regulars and travelers alike for hearty traditional food, malty ales made on the premises, and lively conversation.

 The Shaskeen
MAP M6 ■ 909 Elm St, Manchester
This atmospheric pub was founded by two Irish musicians who put equal effort both into the nightly schedule of traditional Irish music and the classic Irish fare.

 Patrick's Pub & Eatery
MAP M5 ■ 18 Weirs Rd, Gilford
Trivia nights, open mic nights, and Saturday sessions of rotating musical styles create a lively atmosphere at Patrick's. Pints of Guinness complement the Irish-themed menu.

 Barley House
MAP M5 ■ 132 N Main St, Concord
With a dozen fine imported and locally brewed beers on tap and a wood paneled pub room, the Barley House feels more like a private club than a public bar.

⑨ Woodstock Inn Station & Brewery
MAP L4 ■ 135 Main St, North Woodstock
English malts and international hops yield a range of outstanding ales geared for outdoors enthusiasts.

Roaring fire at the Woodstock Inn

⑩ Moat Mountain Smoke House & Brewing Co
MAP M4 ■ 3378 White Mountain Hwy, Rte 16, North Conway
This ski-country restaurant takes barbecue seriously. The brisket is Texas dry rub, the pork comes Carolina-style (vinegar doused), and ribs come St. Louis-style. Match them all with the caramel brown ale.

Restaurants

PRICE CATEGORIES

For a three course meal for one with half a bottle of wine (or equivalent meal), taxes and extra charges.

$ under $40 $$ $40–$65 $$$ over $65

① Ristorante Massimo
MAP N6 ▪ 59 Penhallow St, Portsmouth ▪ 603 436 4000 ▪ Closed L, Sun ▪ $$

Sophisticated, largely northern Italian dishes make great use of New England seafood, especially lobster from local waters. The romantic dining room is set in an authentic Federal-era custom house.

② Black Trumpet Bistro
MAP N6 ▪ 29 Ceres St, Portsmouth ▪ 603 431 0887 ▪ Closed L ▪ $$

The chef-owner transforms local seafood and produce into lusty American bistro dishes.

③ The Restaurant at Burdick's
MAP K6 ▪ 47 Main St, Walpole ▪ 603 756 9058 ▪ Closed Mon, D Sun ▪ $$$

Casual country French dining at this bistro complements the artisanal chocolates sold in the adjoining room.

④ Cotton
MAP M6 ▪ 75 Arms St, Manchester ▪ 603 622 5488 ▪ Closed Sat–Sun L ▪ $$

Start with New Hampshire's best martini, then order from the menu of updated comfort food – meatloaf and mash, steak salad, buttermilk-fried chicken – in this seriously hip spot.

⑤ Luca's Mediterranean Café
MAP L6 ▪ 10 Central Sq, Keene ▪ 603 358 3335 ▪ Closed Apr–Dec: Sat–Sun L; Jan–Mar: Sun ▪ $$

Northern Italian cuisine reigns at this casual but classy trattoria, although specials may be from North Africa and the eastern Mediterranean.

⑥ Hart's Turkey Farm Restaurant
MAP M5 ▪ 233 Daniel Webster Hwy, Rtes 3 & 104, Meredith ▪ 603 279 6212 ▪ $

It's Thanksgiving every day at this family restaurant specializing in roast turkey dinners with all the fixings. You can also get your gobbler as a fricassee or with pasta.

Traditional inn atmosphere, Pine

⑦ Pine
MAP L4 ▪ 2 S Main St, Hanover ▪ 603 646 8000 ▪ $$

At the venerable inn that serves as the center of Dartmouth College's social scene, Pine serves farm-to-table fare with local ingredients.

⑧ Three Chimneys Inn
MAP N6 ▪ 17 Newmarket Rd, Durham ▪ 603 868 7800 ▪ Closed Sun–Mon L ▪ $$

French country cooking is given a strong American accent here.

⑨ The Grazing Room
MAP L5 ▪ 3 The Oaks, Henniker ▪ 603 428 3281 ▪ Closed L; Sun brunch ▪ $$

Located in a romantic country setting, Colby Hill offers stately dining on classic New England dishes.

⑩ Ariana's Restaurant
MAP L4 ▪ 1 Market St, Lyme ▪ 603 795 4824 ▪ Closed Tue ▪ $$

This outstanding farm-to-fork restaurant, housed in an historic inn, serves excellent American fare with Italian flavors.

See map on p114 ←

🔟 Maine

Larger than New Hampshire, Connecticut, Rhode Island, and Vermont combined, Maine is New England on a grand scale. With a coast that wriggles around peninsulas and into harbors for an astonishing 5,500 miles (8,850 km) between Kittery and Calais, there's plenty to see without abandoning the smell of salt air. Turn off Route 1 down any peninsula, and you enter a world of scenic vistas and small villages, with a lobster harbor at the tip. Beaches stretch for miles along Maine's south coast. A province of Massachusetts from 1652 to 1820, Maine was famous well into the 20th century for harvesting timber and building tall ships. Even today, the state's windjammer fleet is one of the world's largest.

The Maine moose

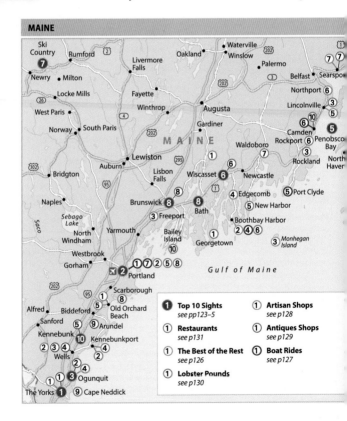

MAINE

Ski Country ⑦ · Rumford · Newry · Milton · Locke Mills · West Paris · Norway · South Paris · Livermore Falls · Fayette · Winthrop · Oakland · Waterville · Winslow · Palermo · Belfast · Searspo · Northport · Lincolnville · Augusta · Gardiner · Camden · Rockport · Penobsco Bay · Waldoboro · Rockland · North Haven · Bridgton · Auburn · Lewiston · Lisbon Falls · Wiscasset · Newcastle · Edgecomb · Port Clyde · Naples · Brunswick · Bath · New Harbor · Sebago Lake · Freeport · Boothbay Harbor · North Windham · Yarmouth · Bailey Island · Georgetown · Monhegan Island · Westbrook · Gorham · Portland · Gulf of Maine · Scarborough · Alfred · Biddeford · Old Orchard Beach · Sanford · Arundel · Kennebunk · Kennebunkport · Wells · Ogunquit · The Yorks · Cape Neddick

❶ **Top 10 Sights** *see pp123–5*		❶ **Artisan Shops** *see p128*	
❶ **Restaurants** *see p131*		❶ **Antiques Shops** *see p129*	
❶ **The Best of the Rest** *see p126*		❶ **Boat Rides** *see p127*	
❶ **Lobster Pounds** *see p130*			

The 41-ft (12-m) tall Nubble Light lighthouse, built in 1879 at Cape Neddick

1 The Yorks

MAP N5, N6 ■ Museums of Old York: 3 Lindsay Rd; 207 363 1756; open late May–early Sep: 10am–5pm Tue–Sat, 1–5pm Sun (early Sep–mid-Oct: closed Mon–Wed); adm; www.oldyork.org

York has two very different faces: the historical York Village and the brassy summer playground of York Beach. Maine's first successful European settlement, York was founded in 1634; the Old York Historical Society chronicles local history. Long Sands and Short Sands swimming beaches are the main draws at York Beach, which also has a carousel and arcade. Drive to the end of Cape Neddick to see iconic Nubble Light.

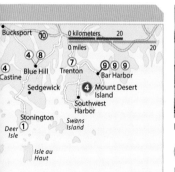

Boats in the harbor at Portland

2 Portland and Casco Bay

Maine's largest community has the cultural advantages of a mid-sized city (see pp28–9) and all the natural beauty of a handsome, well-protected bay. The once-bedraggled maritime area has been reborn in the animated Old Port.

3 Ogunquit

MAP N5

Plein air painters discovered Ogunquit in the 1890s, and visitors have been seeing beauty at every turn since. Picturesque Perkins Cove bristles with art galleries, souvenir shops, and seafood shacks. Marginal Way, a short trail over a rocky headland north of the cove, is lined with profusely blooming beach roses. The path exits onto Ogunquit Beach (see p53).

Mount Desert Island overlooking the waters of Frenchman Bay

4 Mount Desert Island

French explorer Samuel de Champlain pinned the name *Ile des Monts Deserts* on this large island *(see pp14–15)* in 1604, and "island of bare mountains" has stuck ever since. The rocky balds that Champlain observed are prized among hikers and climbers in Acadia National Park.

Pumpkin Island, Penobscot Bay

5 Penobscot Bay
MAP Q3

The west coast of Penobscot Bay is Maine's best-kept secret, although most of the state's windjammers *(see p56)* anchor in Rockland and Camden. Rockland is Maine's lobster capital and home of the treasured Farnsworth Art Museum *(see p45)*; Camden has a beautiful harbor – a yacht-filled silver bowl at the foot of a mountain; Belfast is a community where artisans set the tone.

6 Wiscasset
MAP P4

Even simply driving through, you'll have plenty of time to contemplate Wiscasset's self-description as the "prettiest village in Maine" *(see p48)* because the narrow bridge across the Sheepscot River backs traffic up in midsummer. Better to park and walk around this stunning village where adept 18th- and 19th-century ship-wrights turned their talents to building houses for sea captains.

7 Ski Country
MAP N2

Moist air masses sweeping up the eastern seaboard meet the icy jet stream bringing Arctic air off the Canadian shield in northwest Maine, just east of the White Mountains. The result is massive dumps of snow that guarantee the peaks around Bethel, Newry, Kingfield, and Jackman will be buried in the white gold that skiers crave. In the summertime, long green meadows are transformed into championship golf courses.

8 Bath and Brunswick
MAP P4

Nearly half the US ocean-going sailing vessels launched in the late 19th century went down the ways from Bath shipyards – a history

THE MAINE MOOSE

The official state animal, the moose (*Alces alces*) is found all over Maine, with the greatest concentrations near Moosehead and Rangeley lakes. They often cross roads at dawn and dusk, so take special care driving through swampy areas. An 800-lb (363-kg) gentle giant makes a considerable impact in a collision.

detailed at the Maine Maritime Museum (see p46). Nearby Brunswick is better known for making scholars than ships. Bowdoin College educated authors Nathaniel Hawthorne and Henry Wadsworth Longfellow, as well as intrepid Arctic explorers Robert Peary and Donald MacMillan. The college's Peary-MacMillan Arctic Museum (see p42) displays artifacts and images from their expeditions.

⑨ Moosehead Lake

MAP P1 ▪ Visitor center: 480 Moosehead Lake Rd, Greenville; 207 695 2702; open late May–mid-Oct: 10am–4pm daily (closed Sun & Mon in off-season); www.mooseheadlake.com

The largest body of water contained within a single New England state, from the air, the lake resembles the antlers of a moose, and if you take a seaplane tour, you'll almost certainly see some of these impressive animals out for a swim. The lake is known for hunting, fishing, and winter snowmobiling, but photographic moose safaris are increasingly popular. Inquire at Greenville's visitor center.

⑩ Kennebunk

MAP N5 ▪ Brick Store Museum: 117 Main St, Kennebunk; 207 985 4802; open 10am–5pm Tue–Fri, 10am–4pm Sat; noon–4pm Sun; adm; www.brickstoremuseum.org

The town of Kennebunk developed two distinct villages: Kennebunk on the river, and Kennebunkport where the river meets the ocean. Once a shipbuilding center, Kennebunk has now become principally a community of summer vacation homes. Visit the Brick Store Museum for exhibits on the town's cultural and historic heritage. Then head to Dock Square in Kennebunkport to peruse the boutiques and galleries.

Beach at Kennebunk

A DAY'S DRIVE IN WYETH COUNTRY

▶ MORNING

The rocky Maine coast has entranced many painters, but Andrew Wyeth (1917–2009) was among the few to chart the quiet country life of the saltwater farms. This drive shows you Maine through Wyeth's eyes. From Rte 1 in **Waldoboro**, turn south toward the village of **Friendship**, famed for its namesake sloop. You'll see lots of them in the harbor before continuing north toward **Cushing**. The **Olson House** was made famous in Wyeth's "Christina's World" (1948), and it looks little changed since Wyeth painted it. Continue north to Rte 1, passing through handsome **Thomaston**, and turn right at High St (Rte 131). Enjoy stunning vistas as you drive to **Port Clyde** at the tip of the peninsula, where the Monhegan Island (see p50) ferry departs.

AFTERNOON

North of the harbor, look for signs to **Marshall Point Lighthouse Museum**. The light was automated in 1971; the former keeper's house is a local history museum (see p51). Head north again toward **Tenants Harbor** for dockside lobster at **Luke's** (Commercial St). Continue north to Rockland, to visit the **Maine Lighthouse Museum** (see p47), and spend time at the **Farnsworth Art Museum** (see p45) enjoying art by three generations of Wyeth painters along with the work of modernist Louise Nevelson, who grew up in Rockland.

See map on pp122–3

The Best of the Rest

1 Deer Isle and Stonington
MAP Q3

Artists and fishermen seem to flock together in Maine. The Haystack Mountain School of Crafts made Deer Isle famous years ago, while the lobster boats still tend to out-number pleasure craft in the striking harbor at Stonington.

2 Boothbay Harbor
MAP P4

Regarded by many as the boating capital of midcoast Maine, this pic-turesque harbor is a great spot to go on a whale-watching trip, kayak excursion, or pleasure cruise.

3 Monhegan Island
MAP Q4

Birders and hikers flock to the rocky cliffs of this offshore art colony every summer. After the summer tourists leave, the lobster fishermen return for the profitable winter season.

4 Castine and Blue Hill
MAP Q3, R3

A drive down a single peninsula takes you to two great towns: art-minded Blue Hill, with its excellent pottery studios; and Castine, with its rich Colonial heritage and the Maine Maritime Academy.

5 Old Orchard Beach
MAP N5

This sandy beach, with its gentle surf, is the perfect place for swimming. Kids love the amusement park rides, the waterslide, and the pier with its fast food vendors and games of skill.

6 Lubec and Campobello Island
MAP R2 ■ West Quoddy Head Light Visitor Center: 973 S Lubec Rd ■ 207 733 2180 ■ Open late May–mid-Oct: daily ■ www.westquoddy.com

America's first sunrise strikes the West Quoddy Head in Lubec. A bridge leads to Campobello Island, where Franklin Roosevelt summered.

7 Bangor
MAP Q2

Fine mansions dot this Penobscot River town, once the world's timber capital and today a jumping-off point to the northern wilderness.

8 Baxter State Park
MAP Y5 ■ 64 Balsam Dr, Millinocket (office) ■ 207 723 5140 ■ Closed Sat–Sun mid-Oct–late May ■ Adm ■ www.baxterstatepark authority.com

Test your mettle by scaling 5,267-ft (1,605-m) Mount Katahdin, set in 327 sq miles (848 sq km) of pristine forest.

9 Rangeley Lake Region
MAP N2

Spruce- and hemlock-clad peaks rise with robust grace from a plateau splashed with 112 lakes and ponds – an outdoors enthusiast's paradise.

10 Allagash Wilderness
MAP Y4–5 ■ Maine Bureau of Parks & Lands: 18 Elkins Ln, Augusta ■ 207 287 3821

Forever wild, the Allagash is a legendary system of rivers and lakes where the trout (and the mosquitoes) are bigger than anywhere else.

Old Orchard Beach

Boat Rides

① Casco Bay Lines
MAP N4 ▪ 56 Commercial St, Portland ▪ 207 774 7871 ▪ Ferry year-round; some cruises summer only ▪ Adm ▪ www.cascobaylines.com
Sunrise, sunset, or moonlight cruises on the oldest ferry service in the US.

② Three Rivers Whitewater
MAP P1 ▪ 2265 Rte 201, West Forks ▪ 207 663 2104 ▪ Open May–Oct ▪ Adm ▪ Minimum age 10 ▪ www.threeriverswhitewater.com
Guides negotiate the thrilling waves and rapids on this rafting trip down the Kennebec River in Maine.

③ Bold Coast Charter Company
MAP R2 ▪ Cutler Harbor ▪ Open Jun–mid-Aug ▪ Adm ▪ Reservations essential ▪ www.boldcoast.com
About 10,000 endangered puffins nest on Machias Seal Island. Bold Coast offers sightseeing trips for bird-watchers and photographers.

④ Cap'n Fish's Whale Watch
MAP P4 ▪ 1 Wharf St, Boothbay Harbor ▪ 207 633 3244 ▪ Open late May–mid-Oct ▪ Adm ▪ www.mainwhales.com
A shipboard naturalist will help you identify migrating whales. You might spot seals, porpoises, and dolphins.

⑤ Monhegan Boat Line
MAP Q4 ▪ Port Clyde ▪ 207 372 8848 ▪ Ferry year-round; cruises Jun–Aug ▪ Adm ▪ www.monheganboat.com
Drift past lobster boats on the trip out from Port Clyde to Monhegan Island, or opt for a cruise past the Muscongus Bay lighthouses.

⑥ Schooner Appledore
MAP Q3 ▪ Bayview Landing, Camden ▪ 207 994 8402 ▪ Open Jun–Oct ▪ Adm ▪ www.appledore2.com
Get your sea legs with day sails around Penobscot Bay.

⑦ Portland Schooner Co.
MAP N4 ▪ Maine State Pier, Portland ▪ 207 766 2500 ▪ Open mid-May–Oct ▪ Adm ▪ www.portlandschooner.com
Three historic schooners make two-hour sails through the waters of Casco Bay. Enjoy spotting seals, seabirds, and nonstop views of the rugged coastline.

SS _Katahdin_ on Moosehead Lake

⑧ SS Katahdin
MAP P1 ▪ 12 Lily Bay Rd, Greenville ▪ 207 695 2716 ▪ Open late Jun–mid-Oct ▪ Adm ▪ www.katahdincruises.com
Moosehead Lake is stunning during the fall foliage and there can be no better way to survey the scene than aboard the gloriously preserved SS _Katahdin_, a 1914 steamboat.

⑨ Downeast Windjammer Cruises
MAP R3 ▪ Bar Harbor Inn Pier, Bar Harbor ▪ 207 288 4585 ▪ Open May–Oct ▪ Adm ▪ www.downeastwindjammer.com
Historic schooners and a lobster sloop make day sails through the islands of Frenchman Bay.

⑩ Allagash Canoe Trips
MAP Y5 ▪ Carrabassett ▪ 207 280 1551 ▪ Open May–Sep ▪ Adm ▪ Apply on website ▪ www.allagashcanoetrips.com
The Allagash River and Chamberlain Lake offer paddling journeys in the North Woods wilderness and good trout fishing as well.

See map on pp122–3

Artisan Shops

1 Tandem Glass
MAP P3 ▪ 6 Eagle Lodge Lane, Dresden

Terrill and Charlie Jenkins have been crafting attractive hand blown art glass since 2006, at their saltbox barn studio and gallery, located northwest of Wiscasset.

Weathervanes of Maine

2 Weathervanes of Maine
MAP N5 ▪ 1451 Rte 1, Wells

Weathervanes once topped every Maine barn. This company helps keep the tradition alive, with its menagerie of hand-crafted copper animals, from a jaunty rooster to a flying pig or a dolphin.

3 Thos. Moser Cabinetmakers
MAP P4 ▪ 149 Main St, Freeport

You might pick up some home decorating tips in this restored 19th-century home, where contemporary paintings and photography are displayed next to the cabinetmakers' furniture.

4 Edgecomb Potters Gallery and Studio Complex
MAP P4 ▪ 727 Boothbay Rd, Rte 27S, Edgecomb

Richly colored glazes are the hallmark of Edgecomb porcelain, which is on sale here alongside pieces by other artisans, working in wood, metal, and glass.

5 Maine Artisans
MAP Q3 ▪ 2518 Atlantic Hwy, Lincolnville Beach

Representing the creativity of mid-coast Maine, this cooperative gallery of local artisans sells colorful knitted socks and driftwood lamps, delicate glass orchids, and paintings on slate, among other wares.

6 Swans Island Company
MAP Q3 ▪ 231 Rte 1, Northport

An elegant pure-wool Swans Island blanket is the ultimate word in cold-weather luxury. The Northport showroom-studio is set in a lovely converted 1780s farmhouse.

7 Bluejacket Ship Crafters
MAP Q3 ▪ 160 E Main St, Searsport

The oldest ship-modeling company in the country has more than 100 historically accurate examples on display. Select a kit for a sailing sloop, or radio-controlled lobster boat.

8 Rackliffe Pottery
MAP R3 ▪ 130 Ellsworth Rd, Blue Hill

Stop off at this workshop overlooking Blue Hill Bay and you might see artisans throwing dishware on a potter's wheel. A blueberry bowl makes a perfect souvenir of Maine.

9 Abbe Museum
MAP R3 ▪ 26 Mount Desert St, Rte 3, Bar Harbor

The gift shop of this small museum has highly prized sweetgrass, ash, and birchbark baskets made by Maine's Wabanaki peoples.

10 Columbia Falls Pottery
MAP R2 ▪ 4 Main St, Machias

It seems as if the artists at this pottery simply look out the window for inspiration for their tiles, clocks, lamps, and crocks, all decorated with painted blueberries, lupines, sailboats, and shore birds. Complimentary gift wrap for purchases.

Antiques Shops

1 York Antiques Gallery
MAP N5 ▪ 746 Rte 1, York
Dealers at this gallery specialize in fine 18th- and 19th-century furniture and accessories. You probably won't find a bargain, but you might pick up decorating ideas.

2 Hutchins' Antiques Etc
MAP N5 ▪ 166 Main St, Ogunquit
After a lazy morning on Ogunquit beach, peruse the offerings in this nearby family-owned shop. Dealers lean toward small objects of desire – jewelry, glass, porcelain, linens, and nifty little kitchen items.

3 Douglas N. Harding Rare Books
MAP N5 ▪ 2152 Post Rd, Rte 1, Wells
You'll find volumes on everything from circus arts to UFOs in this 14-room shop with more than 100,000 used and rare books.

4 Smith-Zukas Antiques
MAP N5 ▪ 1755 Post Rd, Rte 1, Wells
Each of the buildings in this inviting complex has a distinctive personality, with an eclectic mix of offerings from formal furnishings to shabby-chic accessories, and architectural ornaments to garden statuary.

Items for sale at Smith-Zukas Antiques

5 Victorian Lighting
MAP N5 ▪ 29 York St, Rte 1, Kennebunk
Despite the name, this illuminating shop carries high-quality lighting fixtures from the 1840s right through to the 1930s, restored and rewired for modern homes. Select a simple sconce or a showpiece chandelier.

6 Marston House Wiscasset
MAP P4 ▪ 101 Main St, Wiscasset
The proprietors grew up in Paris, so the shop's furniture, soft linens, clay pots, wire garden stands, and stoneware serving pieces all have Gallic flair.

7 Pumpkin Patch Antiques
MAP Q3 ▪ 15 Rte 1, Searsport
Country furniture and a lovely selection of mid-20th-century quilts highlight the domestic antiques in this small shop. Nautical items and Chinese porcelain are reminders of Searsport's maritime heyday.

8 Cabot Mill Antiques
MAP P4 ▪ 14 Maine St, Brunswick
This restored brick textile mill has 160 booths that feature folk art, nautical antiques, furniture, art, pottery, and jewelry.

9 Antiques USA
MAP N5 ▪ Rte 1, Arundel
Route 1 from York to Arundel is dense with antiques shops. Antiques USA is one of the largest, bringing hundreds of dealers with different tastes and interests under one roof.

10 Big Chicken Barn Books & Antiques
MAP R3 ▪ 1768 Bucksport Rd, Ellsworth
The proprietors of this gigantic emporium encourage browsers to bring a picnic lunch. It takes hours to peruse the thousands of magazines, rare books, and antiques.

See map on pp122–3

Lobster Pounds

① Five Islands Lobster Co
MAP P4 ▪ 1447 Five Islands Rd, Georgetown ▪ 207 371 2990 ▪ Closed mid-Oct–early May ▪ $

Lobstermen stream in all day as diners at picnic tables crack lobsters, dip the meat in melted butter, and enjoy the view of a perfect harbor.

② The Clam Shack
MAP N5 ▪ On the Bridge, Kennebunkport ▪ 207 967 3321 ▪ Closed mid-Oct–mid-May ▪ $

The namesake fried clams are always good, but the real specialty here is the lobster roll.

The Clam Shack

③ The Lobster Pound
MAP Q3 ▪ 2521 Rte 1, Lincolnville Beach ▪ 207 789 5550 ▪ Closed mid-Oct–mid-May ▪ $

Take a dip, then sit on the deck of this classic seafood restaurant to break down a boiled lobster dinner – or dine inside to escape mendicant gulls.

④ Barnacle Billy's
MAP N5 ▪ 70 Perkins Cove Rd, Ogunquit ▪ 207 646 5575 ▪ Closed Nov–mid-Apr ▪ $

The bargain-hunter's choice in a pricey resort, Billy's has a full-service restaurant and a bare-bones seafood shack on scenic Perkins Cove.

⑤ Shaw's Fish & Lobster Wharf
MAP P4 ▪ 129 Rte 32, New Harbor ▪ 207 677 2200 ▪ Closed mid-Oct–mid-May ▪ $

A lobster fan's nirvana, Shaw's has great views of the harbor, a raw bar, and a full liquor license *(see p67)*.

⑥ Boothbay Lobster Wharf
MAP P4 ▪ 97 Atlantic Ave, Boothbay Harbor ▪ 207 633 4900 ▪ Closed mid-Oct–mid-May ▪ $$

In a legendary lobstering harbor, the Lobster Wharf has the shortest possible distance from trap to plate.

⑦ Trenton Bridge Lobster Pound
MAP R3 ▪ 1237 Bar Harbor Rd, Trenton ▪ 207 667 2977 ▪ Closed mid-Oct–late Apr ▪ $

Lobster, nutcrackers, picks, and heaps of paper napkins are really all you need, and this pound barely on the mainland side from Mount Desert Island is a bargain spot for authentic experiences. BYOB.

⑧ Bayley's Lobster Pound
MAP N5 ▪ 9 Ave 6, Pine Point, Scarborough ▪ 207 883 4571 ▪ Closed mid-Oct–late Apr ▪ $

Founded in 1915, there are some great specialties offered here, like lobster-stuffed mushrooms and excellent crabcakes.

⑨ Cape Neddick Harborside Restaurant
MAP N5 ▪ 60 Shore Rd, Cape Neddick ▪ 207 363 5471 ▪ Ring for winter hours ▪ $$

Sample the steamed mussels or clams first, before cracking into the main attraction on the menu.

Cape Neddick Harborside Restaurant

⑩ Cook's Lobster & Ale House
MAP P4 ▪ 68 Garrison Cove Rd, Bailey Island ▪ 207 833 2818 ▪ $

Enjoy your lobster surrounded on three sides by water, with a view of the world's only crib-stone bridge.

Restaurants

PRICE CATEGORIES

For a three course meal for one with half a bottle of wine (or equivalent meal), taxes and extra charges.

$ under $40 $$ $40–$65 $$$ over $65

1 Dockside
MAP N6 ▪ 22 Harris Island Rd, York ▪ 207 363 2868 ▪ Closed Nov–May ▪ $$

An island location in York Harbor makes fish the natural dish, from haddock, cod, and lobster to diver scallops and clams from nearby beds. Bouillabaisse of Maine seafood is always a good bet.

2 Eventide Oyster Co
MAP N4 ▪ 86 Middle St, Portland ▪ 207 774 8538 ▪ Open L, D daily ▪ $$

Favored by hipsters, this eatery serves an array of fresh oysters and other local delicacies of the sea. An extensive wine list and craft beers are on offer here.

3 Primo Restaurant
MAP Q3 ▪ 2 S Main St, Rockland ▪ 207 596 0770 ▪ Closed L, Tue, ring for winter hours ▪ $$$

The chef here conjures up culinary wonders from mostly home-grown produce – even Brussels sprouts get to be stars in season.

4 White Barn Inn
MAP N5 ▪ 37 Beach Ave, Kennebunkport ▪ 207 967 2321 ▪ Closed L ▪ Reservations essential; jacket required for men ▪ $$$

Two 1820s barns make a surprisingly elegant and restful space in which to enjoy the four-course tasting menu.

5 Cheval
MAP N4 ▪ 58 Pine St, Portland ▪ 207 772 1110 ▪ Open D Tue–Sat ▪ $$

This West End brasserie offers an American menu with French and Spanish accents.

6 Nina June
MAP Q3 ▪ 24 Central St, Rockport ▪ 207 236 8880 ▪ Closed Sun–Tue ▪ $$$

A Mediterranean-style restaurant overlooking the picturesque Rockport harbor.

Neons light up Moody's Diner

7 Moody's Diner
MAP Q3 ▪ 1885 Rte 1, Waldoboro ▪ 207 832 7785 ▪ Open B, L, D daily ▪ $

Vacationers and Mainers rub elbows in this iconic diner. Try the blueberry muffins, or the turkey dinner followed by walnut pie.

8 Fore Street
MAP N4 ▪ 288 Fore St, Portland ▪ 207 775 2717 ▪ Closed L ▪ Reservations essential ▪ $$

Sample the wildly popular wood-oven roasted mussels from a menu built largely around local ingredients.

9 West Street Cafe
MAP R3 ▪ 76 West St, Bar Harbor ▪ 207 288 5242 ▪ Closed Nov–Apr ▪ $$

Bright and casual, West Street is known for the classic trio of corn, lobster, and blueberry pie

10 Natalie's
MAP Q3 ▪ Camden Harbour Inn, 83 Bay View St, Camden ▪ 207 236 7008 ▪ Closed L ▪ $$$

Penobscot Bay seafood and local produce underpin the elegant contemporary regional cooking, offered in 3-course and 7-course menus.

See map on pp122–3 ⟵

Streetsmart

Oak Bluffs' gingerbread cottages,
Martha's Vineyard, Massachusetts

Getting Around

Arriving by Air

Logan International Airport in Boston is the principal gateway airport to New England. Located only 3 miles (5 km) from downtown Boston, Logan is an efficient airport with ample parking. Terminal E handles international arrivals but international departures may take off from other terminals.

The cheapest and quickest method to make your way into the city from Logan International Airport is via the free **MBTA** Silver Line buses that connect the airport to to South Station in downtown Boston. These buses are also accessible for people with specific requirements.

A few international flights also arrive at Connecticut's **Bradley International Airport**. **T.F. Green Airport** in Providence, Rhode Island, and **Manchester Boston Regional Airport** in New Hampshire are used by a few European budget carriers and they often provide the most inexpensive domestic air fares to New England. **Portland Jetport** is a good gateway for domestic airlines.

Rail Travel

Amtrak trains from New York follow two main routes in New England. The Northeast Regional route covers Long Island Sound, Connecticut, and Providence, and continues to Boston's South Station. The Vermonter follows the same route to New Haven, Connecticut, then turns north along the Connecticut River. Amtrack's Downeaster service leaves Boston's North Station with stops in New Hampshire and Maine, ending in Brunswick, Maine.

Bus Travel

Concord Coach Lines serves Maine and New Hampshire. **Peter Pan** has stops in Connecticut, Rhode Island, New Hampshire, and western Massachusetts. Other parts of Massachusetts, such as Cape Cod and the South Shore are served by **Plymouth & Brockton**. **Bolt Bus** runs from Boston to New Haven and New York. **Megabus** serves Portland, Boston, and New York.

Boats and Ferries

The CAT high speed car ferry connects Bar Harbor, Maine, and Yarmouth, Nova Scotia in about 3.5 hours from spring to fall. The **Steamship Authority** and **Hy-Line Cruises** depart Hyannis and Woods Hole, Massachusetts, for Nantucket and Martha's Vineyard islands.

Public Transportation

Very little public transportation in New England is integrated between regions. **RIPTA** (Rhode Island Public Transit Authority) operates an extensive bus service throughout Rhode Island with special beach buses from urban centers in the summer. The **MBTA** (Massachusetts Bay Transportation Authority) operates the subway (known more commonly as the "T") and bus lines in the Metropolitan Boston area as well as commuter rail options stretching north to Newburyport, west to Worcester, and south to Providence, Rhode Island. Safety and hygiene measures, timetables, ticket information, transport maps, and more can be obtained from the websites of individual operators.

City Buses

City bus networks are generally frequent and reliable. In most cities, a single fare applies for all bus travel within city limits. Multiple trip tickets and one-day travel passes are available in major cities. Single-trip tickets can also be bought from the driver when boarding your bus but change is not given so you must pay the exact fare.

In Boston, the MBTA bus system expands the transit network to cover more than 1,000 miles (1,600 km). Buses are often crowded and schedules vary. Two useful sightseeing routes are Haymarket–Charlestown (from near Quincy Market to Bunker Hill) and Harvard–Nubian (from Harvard Square via Massachusetts Avenue to Back Bay and South End to Nubian Square in Roxbury). Public transportation in rural areas is less extensive.

Subway

Boston's combined subway and trolley network, known as the "T", is run by the MBTA. It operates 5am–12:45am daily (from 6am on Sundays). Weekday service is every 3–15 minutes; less frequent at weekends. There are five lines: Red, from south of the city to Cambridge; Green, from the Museum of Science westward into the suburbs; Blue, from near Government Center to Logan International Airport and on to Revere; Orange, linking the northern suburbs to southwest Boston; and Silver, a surface bus that runs from Roxbury to Logan International Airport via South Station.

Maps of Boston's subway system are available at Downtown Crossing MBTA station, or online. Admission to subway stations is via turnstiles into which you insert a paper "Charlie" ticket or tap a plastic "Charlie" card. The plastic cards offer a small discount and are intended largely for residents; details on obtaining one can be found on the MBTA website. The paper "Charlie" ticket can be purchased at any MBTA vending machine. It can be loaded with a single trip ($2.40 subway/$1.70 bus), or a 24-hour pass ($12.75) or 7-day pass ($22.50) and is valid on all subway and bus routes.

Taxis

Due to the popularity of Lyft and Uber ride-hailing services, taxicabs are becoming increasingly scarce, though cabs can be still be picked up at taxi ranks and hotels in larger city centers as well as at airports. Reliable city companies include **Arrow Cab Company**, **ASAP Taxi**, **Boston Cab**, **Cambridge Cabs**, **Metro-Cab**, **Providence Taxi**, and **Vermont Ride Network**.

DIRECTORY

ARRIVING BY AIR

Bradley International Airport (BDL)
MAP C4
■ Windsor Locks, CT
w bradleyairport.com

Logan International Airport (BOS)
MAP F2 ■ Boston, MA
w massport.com

Manchester-Boston Regional Airport (MHT)
MAP M6
■ Manchester, NH
w flymanchester.com

MBTA
w mbta.com

Portland Jetport (PWM)
MAP N4 ■ Portland, ME
w portlandjetport.org

T.F. Green Airport (PVD)
MAP E4 ■ Warwick, (Providence), RI
w pvdairport.com

RAIL TRAVEL

Amtrak
w amtrak.com

BUS TRAVEL

Bolt Bus
w boltbus.com

Concord Coach Lines
w concordcoachlines.com

Megabus
w megabus.com

Peter Pan
w peterpanbus.com

Plymouth & Brockton
w p-b.com

BOATS AND FERRIES

The CAT
w ferries.ca/thecat

Hy-Line Cruises
w hylinecruises.com

Steamship Authority
w steamshipauthority.com

PUBLIC TRANSPORTATION

MBTA
w mbta.com

RIPTA
w ripta.com

TAXIS

Arrow Cab Company (Hartford, CT)
w arrowcabct.com

ASAP Taxi (Portland, ME)
w asaptaxi.net

Boston Cab (Boston, MA)
w bostoncab.us

Cambridge Cabs (Cambridge, MA)
w cambridgecabs.info

MetroCab (Boston, MA)
w boston-cab.com

Providence Taxi (Providence RI)
w providence-taxi.business.site

Vermont Ride Network (Burlington, VT)
w greencabvt.com

Driving

Much of New England's charm is found on the region's scenic open roads and on driving tours during fall-foliage season. Major cities' public transportation systems makes it easy to be without a car, but driving is by far the easiest way to explore beyond urban centers.

Driving to New England

The I-95 superhighway is the main entry to New England from New York and points south. This major highway runs close to the coast through Connecticut, Providence, and Rhode Island to the outskirts of Boston. Circumventing the city, the highway continues up through New Hampshire and Maine. From the north, the two major gateways into New England are I-89 and I-91. The latter crosses from Canada into Vermont, then follows a relatively straight line south along the Vermont/ New Hampshire border, through Massachusetts and Connecticut to New Haven. I-89 starts in northwestern Vermont, then cuts diagonally from Burlington to Concord, New Hampshire, where it links up with I-93 into Boston. The major western points of entry are I-84 and I-90 (toll road) from New York state.

Driving in New England

Driving in Boston, where traffic can be heavy and erratic and parking costly, is not advised. Most New England roads are good, with divided highways connecting most major cities. Winter and early spring driving have their challenges. Snow and ice call for special driving skills, and frost heaves create sidewalk cracks and potholes. Heavy traffic can slow progress on popular roads during peak summer season.

Car Rental

To rent a car in New England you must be at least 21 years old and have a valid credit card. Some rental companies charge an extra fee to drivers under age 25. Major international car rental agencies have outlets at all main airports and in all large towns and cities.

Rules of the Road

Third party insurance is required. Drive on the righthand side of the road, and ensure seat belts are worn at all times by the driver and passengers. Right turns on red (unless otherwise indicated) are allowed after coming to a complete stop. All vehicles must give way to emergency service vehicles, and traffic in both directions must stop for a school bus when signals are flashing. Laws vary on using a mobile phone while driving; err on the side of caution and pull over to call or text.

Speeding will usually result in a fine that should be paid in person if possible – the rental company will otherwise charge hefty additional admin fees. Driving under the influence (DUI) of alcohol is a very serious offence, likely leading to arrest.

Cycling

New England offers many options for cyclists of all ages and abilities. Trails in state parks and national parks forests are perfect off-road riding territory, and most ski resorts permit mountain biking (for a fee) in the summer. The commercial website **Bike New England** has compiled guides and links to cycling in the six states.

Bicycle Hire

Most major cities in New England have urban bike sharing programs, some of which include electrically assisted e-bikes. Boston has **Blue Bikes** and Portland has **Zagster**, while **Lime** can be found in a variety of locations. In all cities and towns, cyclists are expected to stay off pedestrian sidewalks.

In non-urban areas, outfitters who rent canoes and kayaks usually also rent touring and mountain bicycles, and can advise on local touring routes to suit all abilities.

Bike Touring

Several companies operate guided and self-guided bike tours around New England. **VBT** covers much of the region, while **Backroads** and **DuVine** focus on Vermont. **Summerfeet**

Cycling specializes in Maine tours. The **Rails-to-Trails Conservancy** provides information and maps on 1,359 trails along abandoned railroad tracks that have been converted into convenient and accessible paths for cyclists and pedestrians.

Cycle Safety

Helmets and high-visibility clothing are not obligatory but wearing them is strongly advised, especially when cycling on rural roads.

Walking and Hiking

Most New England city centers can be explored on foot. Even Boston is a great walking city: it is compact and most streets are flanked by adequate sidewalks. Several different walking tours are available in Boston, most departing from the Information Center located on Boston Common. There are also many free walking tours offered by the rangers of the **Boston**

National Historical Park, including segments of the Freedom Trail to Charlestown Navy Yard.

Hiking trails criss-cross almost all of New England, with the two most popular being Vermont's 265-mile (426-km) **Long Trail** and the **Appalachian Trail**. The latter stretches from Maine to Georgia and covers around 2,200 miles (3,500 km) in total, but can be broken down into shorter segments for day or multi-day hikes. If going off the beaten path, be sure you have good hiking boots, waterproof outerwear, warm inner clothing, a map, and a compass. Make sure your phone is fully charged but don't count on having cell service in remote areas.

There are a number of companies that can arrange two- to five-day hiking excursions in the beautiful New England countryside. One of the best and most established operators is **The Wayfarers**.

Sailing

Sailing vacations, largely aboard schooner-rigged vessels called windjammers, are popular on the Maine coast. On most of these trips travelers are encouraged to actively participate, helping to rig and haul sails. To take part in such an excursion contact the **Maine Windjammer Association** or **Maine Windjammer Cruises**.

Canoeing and Rafting

The Allagash Waterway in Maine undoubtedly provides the ultimate canoeing adventure in New England, and various outfitters can also arrange white-water river rafting trips *(see p56)* there and elsewhere in the state. Many expert sea kayakers tackle the popular Maine Island Trail from Portland to Machias on their own. Contact the **Maine Island Trail Association** for advice on trip planning.

DIRECTORY

CYCLING

Bike New England
w bikenewengland.com

BICYCLE HIRE

Blue Bikes (Boston)
w bluebikes.com

Lime
w li.me/en-us/home

Zagster (Portland)
w zagster.com

BIKE TOURING

Backroads
w backroads.com

DuVine
w duvine.com

Rails-to-Trails Conservancy
w railstotrails.org

Summerfeet Cycling
w summerfeet.net

VBT
w vbt.com

WALKING AND HIKING

Appalachian Trail
w appalachiantrail.org

Boston National Historical Park
w nps.gov/bost

Long Trail
w greenmountainclub.org/the-long-trail

The Wayfarers
w thewayfarers.com

SAILING

Maine Windjammer Association
w sailmainecoast.com

Maine Windjammer Cruises
w mainewindjammercruises.com

CANOEING AND RAFTING

Maine Island Trail Association
w mita.org

Practical Information

Passports and Visas

For entry requirements, including visas, consult your nearest US embassy or check with the **US Department of State**. All travelers to the US should have a machine-readable biometric passport that is valid for six months longer than their intended period of stay. Citizens of the UK, Australia, New Zealand, and the EU do not need a visa, but must apply to enter in advance via the Electronic System for Travel Authorization (**ESTA**). Applications must be made at least 72 hours before travel, and applicants must have a valid passport and a return airline ticket. Visitors from all other regions will require a visa and passport to enter. Be sure to allow plenty of time for the US border agency's thorough passport and visa checks.

Government Advice

Now more than ever, it is important to consult both your and the US government's advice before traveling. The US Department of State, the **UK Foreign and Commonwealth Office**, and the **Australian Department of Foreign Affairs and Trade** offer the latest information on security, health, and local regulations.

Customs Information

You can find information on the laws relating to goods and currency taken in or out of the US on the **Customs and Border Protection Agency** website. All travelers need to complete a Customs and Border Protection Agency form when crossing the US border.

Insurance

We recommend that you take out a comprehensive insurance policy covering theft, loss of belongings, medical care, cancellations and delays, and read the small print carefully. All medical treatment is private and US health insurers do not have reciprocal arrangements with other countries. Car rental agencies offer vehicle and liability insurance; check your policy before traveling.

Health

New England has a number of acclaimed hospitals should you need medical treatment. The US does not have a government health program, so emergency medical and dental care, though excellent, can be very expensive. Medical travel insurance is highly recommended in order to cover some of the costs related to an accident or sudden illness. The price of basic care at a hospital emergency room can rise incredibly quickly. Should you be in a serious accident, an ambulance will pick you up and charge later.

If you need a prescription dispensed, there are pharmacies (drugstores) in every city in the region, some staying open 24 hours. Ask your hotel for the nearest one. Unless otherwise stated, tap water is safe to drink.

For information about COVID-19 vaccination requirements, consult government advice.

Smoking, Alcohol, and Drugs

Smoking and "vaping" are banned in all public spaces such as bus and train stations, airports, and enclosed areas of bars, cafes, restaurants, and hotels. However, many bars and restaurants have designated outdoor areas where smoking is permitted.

Alcohol may not be sold to or bought for anyone under the age of 21. The drink-drive limit is strictly enforced. Recreational cannabis use is decriminalized in all New England states, and fully legal in Massachusetts, Vermont, and Maine.

ID

Passports are required as ID at airports. (American citizens may use a state driver's license to board domestic flights.) Anyone who looks under 25 may be asked for photo ID to prove their age when buying alcohol or tobacco.

Personal Security

New England is generally safe, but petty crime does take place. Pickpockets work known tourist areas and busy streets. Use your common sense, keep valuables in a safe place, and be alert to your surroundings. Lock your car and always store valuables in the trunk.

If you have anything stolen, report the crime as soon as possible at the nearest police station. Get a copy of the crime report to claim on your insurance. Contact your embassy or consulate immediately if your passport is stolen or in the event of a serious crime or accident.

As a rule, New Englanders are very accepting of all people, regardless of their race, gender or sexuality. The country's abolitionist and women's suffrage movements both started here, and the region was early to support same-sex marriage. In fact, Vermont was the first US state to introduce civil unions in 2000, and Massachusetts became the first state to legalize same-sex marriage in 2004. Today, Boston has the largest LGBTQ+ population in the region, but even small towns are accepting. If you do feel unsafe, the **Safe Space**

Alliance pinpoints your nearest place of refuge.

If you need to phone the emergency hotline number for **fire**, **police**, or an **ambulance**, stay on the line even if you are unable to speak in order to allow the emergency locator system to track you. All emergency calls are free.

Travelers with Specific Requirements

The **Society for Accessible Travel** and **Hospitality and Mobility International** offer information for people with disabilities. Most hotels and restaurants are equipped for wheelchair users, and many outdoor recreation areas have wheelchair-friendly trails and tour buses.

Time Zone

New England is in the Eastern time zone: GMT minus five hours. Daylight saving time (EDT) begins at 2am on the second Sunday in March and reverts to standard time (EST) at 2am on the first Sunday in November. During EDT, the local time is GMT minus four hours.

Money

Money in the US comes in dollars, which are divided into 100 cents. Coins come in denominations of 1, 5, 10, 25, and 50 cents, and 1 dollar. Dollar coins are used mostly to buy from vending machines, while 50-cent pieces are rare. The quarter (the 25-cent piece) is the handiest coin for vending machines and parking meters. Notes (bills) come in denominations of $1, $5, $10, $20, $50, and $100. Small businesses will often decline $50 and $100 bills.

Most establishments accept major credit, debit, and prepaid currency cards. Contactless payments are now widely accepted, but it is always worth carrying some cash for smaller items and tips. Cash machines can be found at banks, airline terminals, train and bus stations, and on main streets in major towns. Waiters will expect to be tipped 15 to 20 per cent of the total bill, hotel porters and housekeeping should be given $1 per bag or day, and you should round up taxi fares to the nearest dollar.

Electrical Appliances

Electrical appliances in the US operate on 110–120 volts, 60 cycles, and use a polarized two-prong plug with flat blades. In order to use non-US single-voltage appliances you will need an adapter and voltage converter, both of which are quite commonly available at airport shops and some department and electrical stores. The majority of laptops and travel appliances are dual-voltage, and many hotels have dual-voltage sockets for electric shavers. US phone systems use an RJ11 connector.

Cell Phones and Wi-Fi

Do not rely on cell phones or other devices for navigation or emergency communications in remote areas such as northern Maine and New Hampshire, where signal can be intermittent.

Many hotels, B&Bs, and motels provide Wi-Fi Internet access for travelers carrying their own devices. Free and open Wi-Fi is also usually found at public libraries and coffee shops, as well as many public parks.

Visitors from outside the US can buy pay-as-you-go SIM cards at airports and most phone stores, which can be used in compatible phones. Some networks also sell basic flip phones (with minutes) for as little as $25 (no paperwork or ID required). Canadian residents can usually upgrade their domestic cell phone plan to extend to the US. Pre-paid phone cards usually offer the best rates for long-distance calls, and are sold in most drugstores.

Postal Services

The majority of post offices are open from 8am to 6pm Monday to Friday and 8am to noon Saturday. Properly stamped letters and packages less than 12 oz (340 g) can be dropped into blue mailboxes. For current rates, see the **US Postal Service** website.

Weather

New England weather can vary quite widely. Daytime temperatures from December through February are usually freezing or even colder, while July and August daytime highs usually exceed 80°F (27°C), accompanied by high humidity. September and October are usually cool and dry, while November and March are chilly and damp. Spring weather ranges from warm sun to windy rain. Northerly areas are generally 10°F (7°C) cooler.

Given the changeable weather, it makes sense to dress in layers, with a sweater or jacket for cool summer evenings. Be sure to pack a folding umbrella, sunglasses, and comfortable walking shoes. In midwinter, a warm coat, scarf, gloves, and a hat that protects your ears are necessities, and boots are advised.

While New England is a year-round destination, tourism is busiest from late June through mid-October, and from around Christmas through to late February in ski country.

Cheaper accommodation can often be found from late April into late May, and late October, but some rural attractions may only be open on weekends at these times of the year.

Opening Hours

Most attractions and stores open daily, but many museums close on Mondays. Museums are typically open from 10am to 6pm on weekdays, from 10am to 5pm on Saturday, and from noon to 5pm on Sunday. Hours and days of opening may be reduced in winter so it is best to check beforehand with the venues. Shops typically open from 9 or 10am and close at 6pm in business districts and at 9 or 10pm in shopping centers (they close at 6pm on the weekend).

Some banks open on Saturday mornings, but outside of the bigger cities many stay closed during weekends.

COVID-19 Increased rates of infection may result in temporary opening hours and/or closures. Always check ahead before visiting museums, attractions and hospitality venues.

Visitor Information

Discover New England focuses on the tourism resources of the six New England states. The **Maine Office of Tourism**, **Massachusetts Office**

of Travel and Tourism, **Vermont Department of Tourism**, **New Hampshire Travel and Tourism**, **Rhode Island Tourism**, and **Connecticut Office of Tourism** each have useful online tourism guides to the region, with a range of helpful resources. The **Greater Boston CVB** (Convention and Visitors Bureau) website also offers useful advice.

Many New England museums, galleries, and attractions offer discounts to students and senior citizens. A valid form of ID is required. Students from abroad should carry an International Student Identity Card (**ISIC**) to claim discounts on hostel accommodation, museums, and theaters. Over-50s should look into buying an **AARP** membership (open to non-Americans), which can provide discounts at hotels and on car rentals.

Responsible Tourism

Long considered one of the US's most environmentally conscious regions, New England continues to gain national acclaim for its forward-thinking initiatives and policies. Forty per cent of the region's energy is from renewable sources; Boston is recognized by the Natural Resources Defense Council as the greenest city on the East Coast; and both Maine and Vermont are national leaders in environmental initiatives. Visitors find it easier than ever to be environmentally aware when touring the area. Recycling facilities are common, and community farmers' markets selling local produce and artisan foodstuffs can be found in every corner of every state.

Language

English is the principal language spoken in New England, although parts of the region near the border with Quebec also speak French.

Taxes and Refunds

It is important to remember that listed prices rarely include applicable taxes. All New England states, with the exception of New Hampshire, levy their own sales tax (usually somewhere between 5 and 8 per cent) All states charge taxes on hotel rooms and restaurant meals, and some cities also have tax surcharges. Since none of these taxes are levied at a national level, international visitors cannot claim refunds.

Accommodation

New England's highly varied accommodations can suit almost all tastes and budgets. During the summer vacation season and during fall foliage, lodgings can sometimes be hard to come by, so it is always best to book in advance. Many lodgings often require a minimum stay of two or three nights during holiday periods, summer high season, or weekends during foliage season. An extensive list of accommodation options can be found on the Discover New England website.

State and local lodging and sales taxes can add as much as 19 per cent to your bill and the charges are inescapable. Resorts often charge 15 to 20 per cent either for staff gratuities or as a "resort fee" for facilities.

Camping in New England is allowed only in sanctioned campgrounds. Government-operated campgrounds in state and national parks and forests tend to operate late May to mid-October, while private campgrounds may extend the season in both directions if the weather cooperates.

DIRECTORY

POSTAL SERVICES

US Postal Service
🌐 usps.com

VISITOR INFORMATION

AARP
🌐 aarp.org

Connecticut Office of Tourism
🌐 ctvisit.com

Discover New England
🌐 discovernewengland.org

Greater Boston CVB
🌐 bostonusa.com

ISIC
🌐 isic.org

Maine Office of Tourism
🌐 visitmaine.com

Massachusetts Office of Travel and Tourism
🌐 massvacation.com

New Hampshire Travel and Tourism
🌐 visitnh.com

Rhode Island Tourism
🌐 visitrhodeisland.com

Vermont Department of Tourism
🌐 vermontvacation.com

Places to Stay

PRICE CATEGORIES
For a standard, double room per night (with breakfast if included), taxes and extra charges.

$ under $175 $$ $175–300 $$$ over $300

Boston Lodgings with Character

Charlesmark Hotel
MAP U5 ▪ 655 Boylston St, Boston, MA 02116 ▪ 617 247 1212 ▪ www.charlesmarkhotel.com ▪ $$
In an 1892 townhouse, the Charlesmark resembles contemporary European urban boutique hotels, with its tiny lobby, compact rooms, and high-concept design. Breakfast is included.

Sonder 907 Main
MAP S3 ▪ 907 Main St, Cambridge, MA 02114 ▪ 617 300 0956 ▪ 907 main.com ▪ $$
Set between the MIT campus and the dining and music scene of Central Square, this boutique lodging has an urban loft feel with its industrial elements and exposed brick. There's also a rooftop deck.

Charles Hotel
MAP F2 ▪ 1 Bennett St, Cambridge, MA 02138 ▪ 617 864 1200 ▪ www.charleshotel.com ▪ $$$
Visiting celebrities and academics love the Charles's hallmark style – a spare modernism softened by homey touches as custom quilts on the beds. The hotel's plaza hosts a lively farmers' market and outdoor dining during summer months.

Fairmont Copley Plaza Hotel
MAP U5 ▪ 138 St James Ave, Boston, MA 02116 ▪ 617 267 5300 ▪ www.fairmont.com/copley-plaza-boston ▪ $$$
All 383 rooms in this Edwardian grande dame on Copley Square in the heart of Back Bay have been renovated, updating the traditional genteel style of dark woods and rich fabrics.

The Godfrey Hotel Boston
MAP W4 ▪ 505 Washington St, Boston, MA 02111 ▪ 617 804 2000 ▪ www.godfreyhotel boston.com ▪ $$$
The cornerstone of Downtown Crossing's revitalization, this boutique gem beautifully combines cutting-edge technology with old-fashioned comfort. It's conveniently close to the Financial District for work or the Theater District for play. Very fast Wi-Fi is included.

Harborside Inn
MAP X3 ▪ 185 State St, Boston, MA 02109 ▪ 617 723 7500 ▪ www.harbor sideinnboston.com ▪ $$$
Housed in a granite former spice warehouse, this boutique hotel is located just steps from the harbor and the Faneuil Hall Marketplace. A Boston travel guide is kept in each room.

The Hotel Veritas
MAP F2 ▪ 1 Remington St, Cambridge, MA 02138 ▪ 617 520 5000 ▪ www.thehotelveritas.com ▪ $$$
This very buttoned-down and soothing 31-room boutique hotel is a short block from Harvard Yard but just far enough from Harvard Square to avoid the bustle and noise. Amenities (including Wi-Fi) are luxe, personal service is tops, but many guest rooms are small.

Liberty Hotel
MAP V3 ▪ 215 Charles St, Boston, MA 02114 ▪ 617 224 4000 ▪ www.liberty hotel.com ▪ $$$
Located at the foot of Beacon Hill, this swanky hotel incorporates the historic granite architecture of the Charles Street Jail with the latest in modern design.

Revere Hotel Boston Common
MAP V4 ▪ 200 Stuart St, Boston, MA 02116 ▪ 617 482 1800 ▪ www.revere hotel.com ▪ $$$
Two blocks from Boston Common at the edge of the Theater District, this contemporary luxury hotel has 356 large rooms decorated in minimalist style. The location is convenient for sight-seeing, but can be noisy at night. Wi-Fi is free.

The Verb Hotel
MAP S5 ▪ 1271 Boylston St, Boston, MA 02115 ▪ 617 566 4500 ▪ www.theverbhotel.com ▪ $$$
Located behind iconic Fenway Park, The Verb

transformed a generic mid-20th-century motel into Boston's rock and roll hotel. With a pitch-perfect millennial vibe, it's a drumstick's throw from Berklee College of Music. Wi-Fi is free.

In-Town Hotels

The Dean Hotel
MAP E4 ▪ 122 Fountain St, Providence, RI 02903 ▪ 401 455 3326 ▪ www.thedeanhotel.com ▪ $$
Contemporary chic with a smirk, the Dean even has red lights in the halls to allude to the 1912 building's bordello history. Now it is the millennials' ideal Downcity business hotel with 52 rooms, a beer hall, coffee and karaoke bars, and free Wi-Fi.

Hotel Portsmouth
MAP N6 ▪ 40 Court St, Portsmouth, NH 03801 ▪ 603 433 1200 ▪ www.thehotelportsmouth.com ▪ $$
Soft contemporary styling in 32 rooms complements the historic Queen Anne brick mansion, which is located just off Market Square. In-room iPads, free Wi-Fi, and iPhone docks in each room keep guests connected. The rate includes parking and light breakfast.

Hotel Providence
MAP E4 ▪ 139 Matthewson St, Providence, RI 02903 ▪ 401 861 8000 ▪ www.hotelprovidence.com ▪ $$
Although Providence has a wealth of boutique hotels, this luxurious yet unpretentious downtown place does an excellent job of mixing traditional formality with contemporary design.

Hotel Salem
MAP F2 ▪ 209 Essex St, Salem, MA 01970 ▪ 781 512 6877 ▪ www.thehotelsalem.com ▪ $$
This contemporary boutique hotel sits in the middle of Salem's Essex Street pedestrian mall, steps away from Peabody Essex Museum. Rooms have refrigerators and USB charging outlets. Fast Wi-Fi is included.

Sheraton Portsmouth Harborside Hotel
MAP N6 ▪ 250 Market St, Portsmouth, NH 03801 ▪ 603 431 2300 ▪ www.sheratonportsmouth.com ▪ $$
Standing two blocks from Market Square and next to the whale-watch and harbor cruise docks, this modern business hotel is equally well suited to the leisure traveler. A redwood sauna, large pool, and an extensive fitness room set it apart from other Portsmouth lodgings.

Six South Street Hotel
MAP L4 ▪ 6 E South St, Hanover, NH 03755 ▪ 603 643 0600 ▪ www.sixsouth.com ▪ $$
Although marketed to families visiting students at Dartmouth, this contemporary boutique hotel is also a good base for touring New Hampshire and Vermont from the upper Connecticut River Valley. There is a lively lounge and restaurant on site. Very fast Wi-Fi is included.

The Study at Yale
MAP C5 ▪ 1157 Chapel St, New Haven, CT 06511 ▪ 203 503 3900 ▪ www.studyatyale.com ▪ $$
Facing the Yale School of Art in the midst of Yale's most striking modern architecture, The Study is almost self-consciously sleek and up-to-date, with flat-screen TV, free Wi-Fi access, and iPod docking station on the clock radio. The main floor includes three walnut-paneled meeting rooms, a bar, and the inspired Heirloom restaurant.

The Attwater
MAP F5 ▪ 22 Liberty St, Newport, RI 02840 ▪ 401 846 7444 ▪ www.theattwater.com ▪ $$$
Located in a residential neighborhood just three blocks away from the waterfront, this 17-room boutique hotel is a breath of fresh air in the often stuffy Newport. All of the fresh rooms are bright and colorful and feature fridges, iPads, free Wi-Fi, and beach bags for a walk to the sands. The room rate includes light breakfast.

The Beatrice
MAP E4 ▪ 90 Westminster St, Providence, RI 02903 ▪ www.thebeatrice.com ▪ $$$
The Beatrice combines Providence's sleek design sensibility with its Italian heritage to create a luxe 47-room hotel for sophisticated travelers. Amenities include linens from Milan, Nespresso coffee makers, and heated toilets. Superchef Ignazio Cipriani helms the hotel restaurant, Bellini.

Hotel on North

MAP B2 ■ 297 North St, Pittsfield, MA 01201 ■ 413 358 4741 ■ www. hotelonnorth.com ■ $$$
The 45 rooms of this boutique hotel in two historic downtown buildings are filled with quirky decor, including furniture made by local artisans. Tech features are cutting-edge, and include very fast, free Wi-Fi. The hotel is great for exploring both the northern and southern Berkshires. The service is attentive without being obsequious.

Hotel Vermont

MAP J3 ■ 41 Cherry St, Burlington, VT 05401 ■ 802 651 0080 ■ hotelvt.com ■ $$$
This stylish downtown hotel features Vermont-made blankets, local craftsmanship, and contemporary artwork. Super-fast Wi-Fi is part of the hotel package, along with multiple ports for recharging mobile gear. DIY laundry facilities are a boon for light travelers. Free bicycles and paid yoga classes available.

Press Hotel, Autograph Collection

MAP N4 ■ 119 Exchange St, Portland, ME 04101 ■ 207 808 8800 ■ www. thepresshotel.com ■ $$$
This newspaper building from the mid-1920s was transformed in 2015 into an upscale Old Port luxury hotel. The 110 spacious guest rooms have over-sized windows, vintage-style writing desks, marble baths, and playful newsroom references. USB and power ports abound, and Wi-Fi is free.

Country Inns (Southern)

Captain Freeman Inn

MAP H4 ■ 15 Breakwater Rd, Brewster, MA 02631 ■ 508 896 7481 ■ www. captainfreemaninn.com ■ $$
Conveniently located, close to Cape Cod, this B&B has 11 rooms and was once a sea captain's home. It has traditional decor with mod-ern amenities such as free Wi-Fi. The full gourmet breakfast is superb.

Deerfield Inn

MAP C2 ■ 81 Main St, Deerfield, MA 01342 ■ 413 774 5587 ■ www. deerfieldinn.com ■ $$
Built in 1884, this country inn sits in the heart of 350-year-old Deerfield. The 24 rooms are all different, but consistently decorated in American Colonial Revival style. Historic Deerfield's museum store is on site.

Fife 'n Drum

MAP B4 ■ 53 N Main St, Kent, CT 06757 ■ 860 927 3509 ■ www.fifen drum.com ■ $$
Eight rooms with vaulted ceilings occupy the main inn next to the Fife 'n Drum restaurant with three more rooms in an adjacent Victorian house. The inn is well-placed for shopping at Kent's upscale stores, galleries, and chocolatier.

The Griswold Inn

MAP D5 ■ 36 Main St, Essex, CT 06426 ■ 860 767 1776 ■ www.griswold inn.com ■ $$
An Essex fixture since 1801, the "Gris" reflects the maritime history of this important port town. Five dining rooms domi-nate the historic structure, leaving the guests to occupy the rooms at Hayden House next door. Breakfast costs extra.

The Inn at Woodstock Hill

MAP D4 ■ 94 Plaine Hill Rd, Woodstock, CT 06281 ■ woodstockhill.net ■ $$
The steeply pitched hip roof, multiple dormers, and white clapboard siding make this 1816 inn a visual emblem of rural New England. All rooms have private baths.

Longfellow's Wayside Inn

MAP E2 ■ 72 Wayside Inn Rd, Sudbury, MA 01776 ■ 978 443 1776 ■ www. wayside.org ■ $$
The oldest operating inn in the US (since 1716), it was made famous by American poet H.W. Longfellow's *Tales of a Wayside Inn*. The bar and dining rooms ooze antique charm.

Old Inn on the Green

MAP B3 ■ 134 Hartsville-New Marlborough Rd, New Marlborough, MA 01230 ■ 413 229 7924 ■ www.oldinn.com ■ $$
The spacious rooms of this circa-1800 inn, with adjacent guesthouse on the picturesque village green, are decorated with country antiques, quilts, and folk art.

Red Lion Inn

MAP B3 ■ 30 Main St, Stockbridge, MA 01262 ■ 413 298 5545 ■ www. redlioninn.com ■ $$
The Red Lion has been welcoming travelers since just before the American Revolution. The current main inn (there are

several guest houses too) is a commodious Victorian structure with a perfect porch for sitting and rocking. The guest rooms are individually decorated and feature antiques. Breakfast is extra.

West Lane Inn
MAP B5 ▪ 22 West Lane, Ridgefield, CT 06877 ▪ 203 438 7323 ▪ www. westlaneinn.com ▪ $$
This spacious, gracious 1849 country inn sits on broad green lawns of a picturesque-perfect colonial town in south-western Connecticut. A wraparound porch invites indolent lazing, but many attractions are nearby. Includes free Wi-Fi and light breakfast. Fireplace rooms are available from October to March.

Bradford-Diamond Norris House
MAP F4 ▪ 474 Hope St, Bristol, RI 02809 ▪ 401 253 6338 ▪ www. bristolbnb.com ▪ $$$
Built in 1792, this Federal house features five elegant en-suite rooms and three working fireplaces.

Country Inns (Northern)

Bethel Inn
MAP N3 ▪ 21 Broad St, Bethel, ME 04217 ▪ 207 824 2175 ▪ www.bethel inn.com ▪ $$
Bethel Inn is not far from Sunday River ski resort. The property includes a main inn (a cluster of four Colonial-style buildings), some townhouses, and a championship golf course. Rates include dinner, golf in summer, and cross-country trail fees in winter.

Grafton Inn
MAP K6 ▪ 92 Main St, Grafton, VT 05146 ▪ 802 234 8718 ▪ www.grafton innvermont.com ▪ $$
An 1801 inn, Grafton offers a variety of rooms and suites (and some guest houses) in a picturesque village. Guests have access to the village tennis court and swimming pond. Dining options include the 1801 Tavern and an adjacent barn pub.

The Hancock Inn
MAP L6 ▪ 33 Main St, Hancock, NH 03449 ▪ 603 525 3318 ▪ www. hancockinn.com ▪ $$
This antique hostelry located in the Monadnock foothills has been operated continuously since 1789. The floorboards creak winsomely, but all rooms have modern facilities.

Inn at Shelburne Farms
MAP J3 ▪ 1611 Harbor Rd, Shelburne, VT 05482 ▪ 802 985 8498 ▪ Closed mid Oct–mid May ▪ www.shelburnefarms. org ▪ $$
This late 19th-century mansion overlooking Lake Champlain is the centerpiece of a historic farm (see p111). The hotel's grounds were designed by Frederick Law Olmsted, known as the father of US landscape architecture.

Jackson House Inn
MAP K5 ▪ 43 Senior Ln, Woodstock, VT 05091 ▪ 800 448 1890 ▪ www. jacksonhouse.com ▪ $$
The rustic Jackson House features five queen-bed rooms in an original 1890 wing of the inn, plus six

expansive suites in a newer addition to the property. The garden-like setting just west of Woodstock village makes this inn a popular spot for weddings.

Newcastle Inn
MAP P4 ▪ 60 River Rd, Newcastle, ME 04553 ▪ 207 563 5685 ▪ www. newcastleinn.com ▪ $$
Located in the Pemaquid peninsula overlooking the Damariscotta River harbor, this country inn is perfectly situated for exploring the midcoast Maine peninsulas. Rooms are spread among main inn, cottage, and former carriage house; some have fireplaces. There's a guests-only pub, as well.

New London Inn
MAP L5 ▪ 353 Main St, New London, NH 03257 ▪ 603 526 2791 ▪ www. thenewlondoninn.com ▪ $$
This Federal-style 1792 inn has been transformed into a chic retreat with boldly artistic rooms. The owners wisely maintained the country-hotel look in all public areas, including the double-decker porch strewn with cozy wicker chairs and rockers.

Swift House Inn
MAP J4 ▪ 25 Stewart Ln, Middlebury, VT 05753 ▪ 802 388 9925 ▪ www. swifthouseinn.com ▪ $$
The rooms are spread across the Federal-era main house, a modernized carriage house, and a gatehouse set on a hill above the college town. Some rooms have fireplaces and whirlpool tubs. Breakfast included.

For a key to hotel price categories see p142

Adair Country Inn

MAP L3 ▪ 80 Guider Lane, Bethlehem, NH 03574 ▪ 603 444 2600 ▪ www.adairinn.com ▪ $$$

Each room in this romantic inn, which is located on a historic estate, is named after a nearby peak of the White Mountains. The setting is perfect for watching wildlife and enjoying the alpine landscape.

Pitcher Inn

MAP K4 ▪ 275 Main St, Warren, VT 05674 ▪ 802 496 6350 ▪ www.pitcherinn.com ▪ $$$

This luxury property features in practically every design magazine owing to its decor. The Trout Room has a bed of real tree trunks, and a river-stone fireplace.

Lakeside Lodgings

Hopkins Inn

MAP B4 ▪ 22 Hopkins Rd, New Preston, CT 06777 ▪ 860 868 7295 ▪ www.thehopkinsinn.com ▪ $

An escape for city folks since 1847, this inn standing on a knoll overlooking the north shore of Lake Waramaug adjoins the Hopkins Vineyard. Winter cross-country skiing rivals the pleasures of summer lakeside idling.

Inn at Smith Cove

MAP M5 ▪ 19 Roberts Rd, Gilford, NH 03249 ▪ 603 293 1111 ▪ www.innatsmithcove.com ▪ $

This Victorian inn with long porches and a gazebo on the dock is located on a charming corner of Lake Winnipesaukee. The tower suite has a bedroom, sitting room, and whirlpool tub.

Inn on Newfound Lake

MAP L5 ▪ 1030 Mayhew Tpk, Rte 3A, Bridgewater, NH 03222 ▪ 603 744 9111 ▪ www.newfoundlake.com ▪ $$

This country stagecoach inn on the Boston to Montreal route has welcomed guests since 1840. Renovation has created a lavish Victorian showpiece.

Purity Spring Resort

MAP M4 ▪ 1251 Eaton Rd, Rte 153, East Madison, NH 03849 ▪ 603 367 8896 ▪ www.purityspring.com ▪ $$

Loons aren't the only repeat visitors to Purity Lake; families come back year after year to this rustic resort founded in the 19th century. In summer they paddle, in winter they ski. Rates generally include three meals daily.

Basin Harbor Club

MAP J4 ▪ 4800 Basin Harbor Rd, Vergennes, VT 05491 ▪ 802 475 2311 ▪ www.basinharbor.com ▪ $$$

Take one of 74 cabins or book a room in the guesthouses to join a resort community at Basin Harbor. Sailing and water-skiing on Lake Champlain (lessons are available) are big summer hits. All meals in summer are included.

Lodge at Moosehead Lake

MAP P1 ▪ 368 Lily Bay Rd, Greenville, ME 04441 ▪ 207 695 4400 ▪ www.lodgeatmooseheadlake.com ▪ $$$

Hand-carved beds and spectacular views of Maine's largest lake enhance the modern comforts on offer here. Birding and moose-watching add to the wilderness experience. All rooms are equipped with a private bathroom, while some also have a balcony.

Coastal Lodgings

Wellfleet Motel and Lodge

MAP H4 ▪ 170 Rte 6, South Wellfleet, MA 02663 ▪ 508 349 3535 ▪ late Apr–early Nov ▪ www.wellfleetmotel.com ▪ $

Its location at the north end of the Cape Cod Rail Trail and across Rte 6 from the Audubon wildlife sanctuary is key, but so is the hospitality at this hybrid property of motel and lodge rooms. Many rooms have private patios or balconies overlooking a landscaped courtyard. Breakfast is included.

Atlantic Inn

MAP E6 ▪ High St, Old Harbor, Block Island ▪ 401 466 5883 ▪ late Apr–Oct ▪ www.atlanticinn.com ▪ $$

This 22-room Victorian inn with an acclaimed restaurant is just across the street from Block Island's best bathing beach. The expansive hillside property is dotted with stunning gardens.

Edgewater Motor Inn

MAP N5 ▪ 57 West Grand Ave, Old Orchard Beach, ME 04064 ▪ 207 934 2221 ▪ www.theedgewatermotorinn.com ▪ $$

Five blocks west of the pier at Old Orchard Beach (see p126), this fabulously updated motel with a wide variety of rooms in different sizes stays open all year. No breakfast.

Inn at Castle Hill

MAP F2 ▪ 280 Argilla Rd, Ipswich, MA 01938 ▪ 978 412 2555 ▪ Apr–Dec ▪ www.theinnatcastlehill. com ▪ $$

Understated elegance and serenity characterize this tranquil inn on the Crane Estate. Walk to Crane Beach (see p52) backed by rolling sand dunes.

Shore Acres

MAP J2 ▪ 237 Shore Acres Dr, North Hero Island, VT ▪ 802 372 8722 ▪ www. shoreacres.com ▪ $$

Watch the sun rise through morning mist on Lake Champlain from one of 19 lakeside rooms or four garden-house rooms a short walk away.

Vineyard Harbor Motel

MAP G5 ▪ 60 Beach Rd, Vineyard Haven, MA 02568 ▪ 508 693 3334 ▪ vineyardharbormotel. us ▪ $$

The 40 rooms of this annually refreshed motel share a small private beach owing to its location on the harbor in Vineyard Haven. Every room has a refrigerator and some even have full kitchens. It's on the island bus route and a 10-minute walk from the ferry dock.

Atlantic Oceanside

MAP R3 ▪ 119 Eden St, Rte 3, Bar Harbor, ME 04609 ▪ 207 288 5801 ▪ www.barharbormaine hotel.com ▪ $$$

Set near the entrance to Acadia National Park (see pp14–15), the 12-acre (4.5-ha) former estate of Klondike billionaire Sir Harry Oakes holds

a 153-room resort with jaw-dropping vistas of Maine's rugged coast-line. Guests also benefit from indoor and outdoor swimming pools and a spa.

The Boathouse Waterfront Hotel

MAP N5 ▪ 21 Ocean Ave, Kennebunkport, ME 04046 ▪ 207 967 8223 ▪ www.boathouseme. com ▪ $$$

Just steps from bustling Dock Square, this intimate waterfront hotel has 25 rooms, some with balconies looking out over the water, spread across two buildings. The rooms feature nautical elements, and have iPod docking sta-tions and free Wi-Fi.

Camden Harbour Inn, Camden

MAP Q3 ▪ 83 Bayview St, Camden, ME 04843 ▪ 207 236 4200 ▪ www.camden harbourinn.com ▪ $$$

This romantic luxury boutique hotel located atop a hill pampers its guests with posh rooms, harbor views, wraparound porch, and Natalie's, one of the best fine-dining restaurants in Maine. Breakfast is extra.

Cliff Lodge

MAP H5 ▪ 9 Cliff Rd, Nantucket, MA 02554 ▪ 508 228 9480 ▪ www. clifflodgenantucket.com ▪ $$$

The 12 airy rooms in this 1771 whalemaster's eyrie above Nantucket Harbor embody a style that's half Old Nantucket, half Ralph Lauren. The lodge's rooftop is a great vantage point for watching the sunset.

Edgartown Inn

MAP G5 ▪ 56 North Water St, Edgartown, Martha's Vineyard, MA 02539 ▪ 508 627 4794 ▪ Apr–Oct ▪ www.theedgartown collection.com ▪ $$$

With its white clapboards, cedar shingles, and large front porch, this 1798 sea captain's home is an iconic piece of Edgartown architecture.

Island Inn

MAP Q4 ▪ Monhegan Island, ME 04852 ▪ 207 596 0371 ▪ late May–mid-Oct ▪ www.islandinn monhegan.com ▪ $$$

This 1816 inn above the ferry landing has some of the best views. Half the 32 rooms and suites have pri-vate baths but there's no TV or phones, and cell-phone coverage is poor – which makes the inn a great getaway spot.

Steamboat Inn

MAP D5 ▪ 73 Steamboat Wharf, Mystic, CT 06355 ▪ 860 536 8300 ▪ www. steamboatinnmystic.com ▪ $$$

With each room named for a vessel from Mystic's sailing heyday, this quirky, 11-room riverside inn by the celebrated drawbridge is as nautical as it gets. Evening sherry and cookies are served.

Weekapaug Inn Westerly

MAP E5 ▪ 125 Spray Rd, Westerly, RI 02891 ▪ 401 637 7600, 855 679 2995 ▪ weekapauginn.com ▪ $$$

Set on a barrier beach, this resort features airy rooms and suites with marble baths and feather-top beds. The restaurant uses fresh, local produce.

For a key to hotel price categories see p142

Mountain Lodgings

Birch Ridge Inn

MAP K5 ▪ 37 Butler Rd,
Killington, VT 05751
▪ 802 422 4293 ▪ www.
birchridge.com ▪ $
Located just a mile from
Killington's slopes, this
B&B has 10 contemporary
guest rooms in a double
A-frame lodge. Packages
can cover lift tickets in
winter and tee times in
summer at nearby
Killington Golf Resort.
Popular for weddings.

Inn at Sunset Hill

MAP L3 ▪ 231 Sunset Hill
Rd, Sugar Hill, NH ▪ 603
823 5522 ▪ www.innat
sunsethill.com ▪ $
This country inn and
adjacent farmhouse sit
right outside Franconia
Notch State Park. The
inn offers a genteel base
for winter activities in the
White Mountains.

North Conway Mountain Inn

MAP M4 ▪ 2114 White
Mountain Hwy, N
Conway, NH 03860 ▪ 603
356 2803 ▪ www.north
conwaymountaininn.com
▪ $
With White Mountain
within walking distance
of the local village, this
inn is a perfect base for
hikers and skiers.

Mountain View Grand Resort & Spa

MAP L3 ▪ 101 Mountain
View Rd, Whitefield, NH
03598 ▪ 866 484 3843
www.mountainviewgrand.
com ▪ $$
This venerable hotel
earns its name with
stunning mountain
views in two directions.
It's perfect for both day
hikers and alpine skiers.

Stoweflake Mountain Resort & Spa

MAP K3 ▪ 1746 Mountain
Rd, Stowe, VT 05672
▪ 802 253 7355 ▪ www.
stoweflake.com ▪ $$
Set halfway up the access
highway to the ski-and-
hiking mecca of Mount
Mansfield (see p54),
Stoweflake is the luxury
choice in sports-crazed
Stowe. Choose from
gracious modern hotel
or A-frame townhouses.

West Dover Inn

MAP K6 ▪ 100 Route 100,
West Dover, VT 05356
▪ 802 464 5207 ▪ www.
westdoverinn.com ▪ $$
Close to the Mount Snow
ski area, this historic inn
was originally built in
1846 as a stage coach
stop and tavern. Today,
it has 11 deluxe rooms
well-equipped with
modern amenities. The
tavern is known for its
craft beers.

Equinox Resort & Spa

MAP K6 ▪ 3567 Main St,
Rte 7A, Manchester, VT
05254 ▪ 802 362 4700
▪ www.equinoxresort.
com ▪ $$$
Spacious, country-style
rooms dot four buildings
of this 18th-century resort
with amazing mountain
views. Outdoor activities
on offer include boating,
falconry, golf, fly-fishing,
shooting, winter snow-
mobiling, and skiing.

Mountain Top Inn & Resort

MAP K4 ▪ 195 Mountain
Top Rd, Chittendon VT
05737 ▪ 802 483 2311
▪ www.mountaintopinn.
com ▪ $$$
A true four-season resort
with Nordic ski and
snowshoe trails in winter,
canoes and kayaks in
summer. A choice of
rustic-chic lodge rooms,
cabins, or guesthouse
make Mountain Top a
splendid alpine getaway
without the ski crowds.

Mount Washington Hotel & Resort

MAP M3 ▪ Rte 302,
Bretton Woods, NH 03575
▪ 603 278 1000 ▪ www.
brettonwoods.com ▪ $$$
This palatial hotel offers
upcountry elegance in a
dramatic natural setting.
In summer, golf is the
main lure; in winter, it's
skiing and dogsledding.
The most popular pack-
age includes breakfast
and dinner at any of the
resort's five restaurants.

Trapp Family Lodge

MAP K3 ▪ 700 Trapp Hill
Rd, Stowe, VT 05672
▪ 802 253 8511 ▪ www.
trappfamily.com ▪ $$$
This world-famous resort
on the vast property of
the family that inspired
The Sound of Music has
a large Austrian-style
main lodge and 100
guesthouses. The cross-
country ski trail is
among the best in the
US. Breakfast is extra.

Woodstock Inn & Resort

MAP K5 ▪ 14 The Green,
Woodstock, VT 05091
▪ 802 457 1100 ▪ www.
woodstockinn.com ▪ $$$
The Rockefellers built
this huge modern pile
to look as if it had been
on the town green for
centuries. Rooms
have every conceivable
comfort, but you'll find
it hard to leave the
lobby with its massive
fieldstone fireplace.

Budget-Friendly Lodgings

Bascom Lodge
MAP B2 ■ M. Greylock Summit, Adams MA 01220 ■ 413 743 1591 ■ late May–mid Oct ■ www.bascomlodge.net ■ $
Built in the 1930s on the summit of Mount Greylock as a shelter for hikers on the Appalachian Trail, this lodge has dormitory bunks as well as a few private rooms. Breakfast and dinner are served family style.

Colonial Gables Oceanfront Village
MAP Q3 ■ 7 Eagle Ln, Belfast, ME 04915 ■ 207 338 4000 ■ May–Oct ■ www.colonialgables.com ■ $
Small cottages dot a hillside sloping down to a private beach on Penobscot Bay. Each of the cottages have their own kitchens and front porches. The property also has 13 motel rooms.

East Wind Inn
MAP Q4 ■ Mechanic St, Tenants Harbor, ME 04860 ■ 207 372 6366 ■ May–Oct ■ www.eastwindinn.com ■ $
Wake to lobster boats heading out to haul their catch at this inn located in Tenants Harbor. Rooms are furnished with a mix of country furniture and local antiques. Some of the 26 rooms share baths. TVs available on request in most rooms.

Herbert Grand Hotel
MAP N2 ■ 246 Main St, Kingfield, ME 04947 ■ 207 265 2000 ■ www.herbertgrandhotel.com ■ $
Step back to 1918 at this marvelously old-fashioned mountain hotel close to Sugarloaf skiing and golf. Renovated in 2016, the 26 guest rooms are small, but all have private baths. The terrace over the portico serves as an evening social center.

The Inn at Long Trail
MAP K5 ■ 709 Rte 4, Sherburne Pass, Killington, VT 05751 ■ 802 775 7181 ■ www.innatlongtrail.com ■ $
Hikers adore this rustic lodge at the intersection of the Appalachian and Long trails in the heart of the Green Mountains. (There's a mail drop for through-hikers.) Vermont skiers also flock here. There's an Irish pub on site (see p112).

Kancamagus Swift River Inn
MAP M4 ■ 1316 Kancamagus Hwy, Albany, NH 03818 ■ 603 447 2332 ■ www.swiftriverinn.com ■ $
One of the rare lodgings on the Kancamagus Highway (see p60), this inn offers 10 spacious rooms with eclectic decor. North Conway shopping and White Mountain National Forest trails are nearby.

The Latchis Hotel & Theatre
MAP K6 ■ 50 Main St, Brattleboro, VT 05301 ■ 802 254 6300 ■ www.latchis.com ■ $
The Latchis Hotel is one of only two remaining Art Deco buildings in Vermont. It has modest rooms, free Wi-Fi, and a three-screen theater showing art and independent films.

Sandy Neck Motel
MAP G4 ■ 669 Rte 6A, Sandwich, MA 02537 ■ 508 362 3992 ■ Apr–Nov ■ www.sandyneck.com ■ $
This charming and well-kept older motel is sited at the entrance to the extensive sand bar of Sandy Neck Beach, near the tidal marshes famous for birding. No breakfast.

Breezeway Resort
MAP E5 ■ 70 Winnapaug Rd, Misquamicut, RI 02891 ■ 401 348 8953 ■ May–mid-Oct ■ www.breezewayresort.com ■ $$
Westerly's Misquamicut Beach (see p52) is a short walk from this family-friendly motel and apartment complex where every room has a refrigerator and some have cooking facilities. Guests can also use the outdoor pool and private beach area.

Days Inn
MAP B3 ■ 372 Main St, Great Barrington, MA 01230 ■ 413 528 3150 ■ www.daysinn.com ■ $$
This chain motel with spacious rooms is right at the southern edge of town. It makes an excellent base for foraging for antiques in nearby South Egremont and Sheffield.

Starlight Inn
MAP J3 ■ 5179 Porters Point Rd, Colchester, VT 05446 ■ 802 899 4994 ■ www.starlightinnvt.com ■ $$
The decor in each of the 11 rooms in this modern motel has a Hollywood theme. Guests visiting from May to October get a free pass to the adjacent four-screen Sunset Drive-in.

For a key to hotel price categories see p142

General Index

Acknowledgments

Author

Between them, Patricia Harris and David Lyon have experienced New England from the ground up, working such varied jobs as a commercial fisherman, travel tour leader, arts administrator, and restaurant line cook. They have lived in four New England states and traveled relentlessly in all six. In addition to co-authoring more than two dozen books, they write about travel, food, fine arts, and popular culture for magazines, newspapers, and websites, including HungryTravelers.com. They co-wrote DK's *Eyewitness Travel Guide to Boston* and *Top 10 Boston*.

Publishing Director Georgina Dee
Publisher Vivien Antwi
Design Director Phil Ormerod
Editorial Ankita Awasthi Tröger, Michelle Crane, Rachel Fox, Bharti Karakoti, Freddie Marriage, Alison McGill, Sally Schafer, Farah Sheikh, Jackie Staddon
Cover Design Maxine Pedliham, Vinita Venugopal
Design Tessa Bindloss, Richard Czapnik, Marisa Renzullo
Commissioned Photography Alan Briere, David Lyons, Rough Guides/Dan Banniste, / Susannah Sayler, Tony Souter.
Picture Research Susie Peachey, Ellen Root, Lucy Sienkowska, Oran Tarjan.
Cartography Dominic Beddow, Subhashree Bharti, Simonetta Giori, James Macdonald
DTP Jason Little
Production Nancy-Jane Maun
Factchecker Patricia Harris, David Lyon
Proofreader Kathryn Glendenning
Indexer Hilary Bird
Revisions Elspeth Beidas, Parnika Bagla, Subhashree Bharati, Meghna, Patricia Harris, Sumita Khatwani, Shikha Kulkarni, Suresh Kumar, David Lyon, Bandana Paul, Beverly Smart, Azeem Siddiqui, Priyanka Thakur, Stuti Tiwari, Vaishali Vashisht, Tanveer Zaidi

First edition created by Coppermill Books, London

Picture Credits

The publisher would like to thank the following for their kind permission to reproduce their photographs:
Key: a-above; b-below/bottom; c-centre; f-far; l-left; r-right; t-top

123RF.com: edella 96–7; Felix Lipov 107br; Juli Scalzi 86tl; serezniy 97bl.

Abbe Museum: Ganessa Bryant 15clb. **Abbott's Lobster in the Rough:** 67tr. **Alamy Stock Photo:** age fotostock / Steve Dunwell 71cl; age fotostock/ Terrance Klassen 21br; Katharine Andriotis 103tr; Arcaid Images/Lucinda Lambton 28cl; Bill Bachmann 11cl; Norman Barrett 97cl; Vicki Beaver 76tl; David Brownell 31clb; Cal Sport Media/John Green 61tr; Chris Cameron 30–31; Ken Clare 90cla;
Thornton Cohen 19tl; Alan Copson 3tl, 74–5; Ian G Dagnall 4clb, 30bl, 33tl; Daniel Dempster Photography 37clb; DanitaDelimont.com/Cindy Miller Hopkins 64tr, /Walter Bibikow 17clb; Christian Delbert 58–9; Randy Duchaine100bl, 128cla; EcoPhotography.com/Jerry and Marcy Monkman 27cr; Norman Eggert 11tr; Kevin Galvin 55tr; Granger; NYC. 36clb; hemis.fr / Philippe Renault 125br; Clarence Holmes Photography 14br; Andre Jenny 56br, 114tl; Mark Klein 117cl; David Litschel 131cra; David Lyons 27tl; Terry Mathews 61cl; Henk Meijer 2tl, 8–9; Mira 3tr, 18br, 115b, 132–3; MiraMira 18–19, 109tl; Nikreates 13tc; nobleIMAGES/David Noble 4crb, 51cl; George Ostertag 60br; Pat & Chuck Blackley 53cr; Susan Pease 108clb; Major Pix 88tl; George Robinson 71br; Pierre Rochon 129bl; Stephen Saks Photography 68tl; Kumar Sriskandan 49b; Stan Tess 53bl, 63tr, 73br; Steve Tulley 2tr, 34–5; Frank Vetere 31tl; Freddy Boom Boom Washington 21tl; ZUMApress.comSouthcreek Global/Geoff Bolte 71tr. **AWL Images:** Demetrio Carrasco 4cl; Danita Delimont Stock 22–3, 55br.

Banyan Bar + Refuge: 83b.**Barbara Lynch Gruppo:** Brian Samuels 84tr; WEC Photos 66cl.**Boston Symphony Orchestra:** Hilary Scot 33br.

Cabot Creamery: 111br. **Cape Neddick Lobster Pound:** 130crb. **Center for Historic Shipwreck Preservation:** Kenneth Garrett 47c. **The Clam Shack:** Daryl Getman 130ca. **Craigie On Main:** 66tr.

Discover New England: Connecticut Office of Tourism /Kindra Clineff 95crb, 99crb, /Robert Cregson 96tl; Maine Office of Tourism 104–5, 122cla, /Steve Bly 123cr; New Hampshire Division of Travel and Tourism Development 115tr; Phil Savignano 124t; Vermont Department of Tourism & Marketing 106tr, 107t; Yale University Art Gallery/ Michael Marsland 96tl. **Dreamstime.com:** Alpegor 10cl; Alwoodphoto 51tr; Americanspirit 94tl; Xavier Ascanio 54cra; Jon Bilous 4t,12–13, 20clb, 20–21, 52t; Paul Brady 88br; Chrissieracki 11bl,116t; Angel Claudio 16–17; Cllhnstev 48bl; Ken Cole 14–15; Jerry Coli 4b, 92bl; Christian Delbert 28–9; Songquan Deng 11cra; Eric Broder Van Dyke 29tl; Fashionstock.com 11cla; Stephen Gass 80b; Vlad Ghiea 15tl; Pierrette Guertin 79cl; Jeffrey Holcombe 24–5; Wangkun Jia 28br,108br, 116bl, 123t; Brian Kushner 25tl; Chee-onn Leong 126b; Daniel Logan 87cr; Maglara 77tl; Giuseppe Di Paolo 78b; Sean Pavone 87t; Peanutroaster 118bl; Rolf52 77crb; Jorge Salcedo 10cla; Lee Snider 25bl, 26bc, 48tr; Suchan 38b; Vividrange 12br; Lei Xu 98cl; Colin Young 32cla.

Farnsworth Art Museum: Gift of Mr. and Mrs. Charles Shipman Payson *Romance of Autumn* (1916) George Bellows Oil on canvas 34¼ x 49⅝ inches, 1964.1366 45cl. **Freedom Trail Foundation:** 70c. **Frosty Drew Nature Center & Observatory:** 89cl. **Getty Images:** AFP/Cesar Rangel 45tr; Bloomberg/Herb Swanson 65tr; Boston Globe / Jessica Rinaldi 84clb; Boston Red Sox / Billie Weiss 7cr; Buyenlarge/Carol M. Highsmith 50–51; Education Images 36tr; Brian D. Kersey 69tr; Jack Mitchell 41tr; Portland Press Herald/John Ewing 127cra; Ron Thomas 26–7; Barry Winiker 17cr. **Green Mountain Club:** Jocelyn Hebert 60tl. **Green River Festival:** Flora Reed 73tl.

Harbour House: Tom Bombria 102b. **Harvard Art Museums:** 42tc. **The Hawthorne:** Gustav Holland 84cl.

Isabella Stewart Gardner Museum: Nic Lehoux 40tl.

iStockphoto.com: SeanPavonePhoto 1.

John F. Kennedy Library Foundation: 44cla.

courtesy of Lake Champlain Chocolates: 111ca.

Max Restaurant Group: Photo Credit: LibbyVision.com 101tl. **Montshire Museum:** 110tl. **The Mount, Lenox, MA:** John Seakwood 44hr. **Photograph © 2011 Museum of Fine Arts, Boston:** 40br. **Mystic Seaport, Mystic, CT:** 46b.

courtesy of the Nantucket Historical Association: Peter Vanderwarker 46tl. **National Parks Service:** 4cr. **New England Aquarium:** Webb Chappell 63cl. **Newport Jazz Festival:** Douglas Mason 72b. **Photo courtesy of Norman Rockwell Museum, Stockbridge, Massachusetts:** 32clb.

Oakes & Evelyn: 113cr. **Ocean House:** 93b. **Omni Mount Washington Resort:** 56br.

Peter Pots Pottery: 91c. **Pilgrim Hall Museum:** 78ca. **Prohibition Pig:** Prohibition Pig 112ca.

Ramblewild: 62tl. **Rex by Shutterstock:** Stock Connection 10br; ZUMA Wire/Ricky Bassman 37tr. **Courtesy of the RISD Museum:** 91tl, Bequest of Mrs. Edith Stuyvesant Vanderbilt Gerry *Le Repos* [Repose] (ca. 1870–1871) Édouard Manet 43tl. **Robert Harding Picture Library:** Alan Copson 54clb; Robert Francis 18clb. **Roger Williams Park Zoo:** 62br.

Sandwich Glass Museum: 82c. **Shelburne Farms:** Vera Chang 66br. **Shutterstock.com:** Geoffrey Kuchera 124cl. **The Silver Fork:** Ali Kaukas 112clb. **Sledventures:** 119cr. **Sugarloaf Mountain:** Jamie Walter 57cla. **Sunday River Resort:** Shelley Bowen 4cla; Dave Pecunies 56tl. **SuperStock:** age fotostock/Jannis Werner 13cr, / John Greim 11crb, 16ca; Food and Drink/Tim Hill 65cl; imageBROKER 10cb; Travel Library Limited 24clb.

Wadsworth Atheneum: 41cl. **Williamstown Theatre Festival:** T Charles Erickson Photography 81cla. **Woodstock Inn, Station & Brewery:** John W. Hession 120crb. **Wright Museum of World War II:** 118ca.

Yale University Art Gallery: Elizabeth Felicella 70bl; Michael Marsland 42bl.

Cover
Front and spine: **iStockphoto.com:** SeanPavonePhoto.

Back: **iStockphoto.com:** SeanPavonePhoto b; **Dreamstime.com:** Chee-onn Leong crb, Rixie cla, Marcio Silva tr; **Getty Images:** Jared Alden tl.

Pull Out Map Cover
iStockphoto.com: SeanPavonePhoto.

All other images © Dorling Kindersley

For further information see: www.dkimages.com

Penguin Random House

First edition 2010

First published in Great Britain by Dorling Kindersley Limited, DK, One Embassy Gardens, 8 Viaduct Gardens, London SW11 7BW, UK

The authorised representative in the EEA is Dorling Kindersley Verlag GmbH. Arnultstr. 124, 80636 Munich, Germany

Published in the United States by DK US, 1450 Broadway, Suite 801, New York, NY 10018, USA

Copyright 2010, 2022 © Dorling Kindersley Limited

A Penguin Random House Company

21 22 23 24 10 9 8 7 6 5 4 3 2 1

Reprinted with revisions 2012, 2014, 2017, 2019, 2022

A CIP catalog record is available from the British Library

A catalog record for this book is available from the Library of Congress.

ISSN 1479-344X

ISBN 978 0 2414 7400 6

Printed and bound in China

www.dk.com

As a guide to abbreviations in visitor information blocks: **Adm** = admission charge; **B** = breakfast; **D** = dinner; **L** = lunch.

MIX
Paper from responsible sources
FSC™ C018179

This book was made with Forest Stewardship Council ™ certified paper – one small step in DK's commitment to a sustainable future. For more information go to www.dk.com/our-green-pledge

New England: Selected Index of Places